How to DRAG RACE

Kevin McKenna

CarTech®

Edited by: Paul Johnson
Designed by: Monica Bahr

ISBN-13 978-1-61325-072-3

Printed in USA
Item SA136P

CarTech®
39966 Grand Avenue
North Branch, MN 55056
Telephone (651) 277-1200 • (800) 551-4754 • Fax: (651) 277-1203
www.cartechbooks.com

Back Cover Photos

Top left:
At the race track, a burnout isn't performed for show or fun. A burnout improves traction in your lane, cleans off the tire surface, and puts some heat into the skins. Performed properly, a burnout will not only help improve your car's performance, but it will also help to produce consistent ETs, a must for bracket racing.

Top right:
In order to prevent a frantic thrash at the race track, it's often best to perform most of the maintenance on your vehicle while it's at home or in a well-equipped garage. You should complete regular maintenance routines and tuning procedures before you bring the car to the race track.

Middle left:
Stage: Slowly roll forward a few more inches to light the second stage bulb. The wheel and tire have now blocked both beams. The car is now fully staged and is in position to launch. At this point, a driver needs to be prepared to race and should be focused on the Christmas tree lights. When both lanes are fully staged, that is a signal to the starter to throw the switch that activates the Christmas tree lights. At this point, you should be completely focused on the lights in your lane.

Middle right:
Highly advanced weather stations transmit current conditions to hand-weld wireless receivers in the car, so drivers can make last-second adjustments prior to a run.

Bottom left:
The interior features comfortable seats, as well as a dash-mounted delay box and air shifter. There is also a complete stereo system with MP3 player. A full roll cage and twin safety harnesses help keep both driver and passenger safe.

Bottom right:
Driver skill, including the ability to produce competitive reaction times and properly judge opponents at the finish line, is often the difference between winning and just running in ET bracket racing.

CONTENTS

DEDICATION

To my wife, Jill, my family, and the crew at *National DRAGSTER*, thanks for all the support. It means the world to me.

ACKNOWLEDGMENTS

I'm simply a writer who happens to love drag racing. The real experts who made this book possible are Evan Smith, Bret Kepner, Bob Frey, Frank Hawley, Jack Beckman, Les Garbicz, Dan Fletcher, and Sal and Peter Biondo, all of whom contributed greatly to this project.

INTRODUCTION

It doesn't matter whether you're a veteran drag racer or just starting out, the objective of this book is to make you a better racer. Together, I'm confident that we can achieve that goal. Like any other competitive endeavor, success in drag racing doesn't come easily. If you want to win races, it's going to take a lot of hard work, dedication, and occasionally a bit of good luck.

I've tried to pack as much information as possible into the pages of this book. I've covered every topic from the fundamentals of driving to learning how to properly perform a burnout, setting up your vehicle, selecting essential safety equipment, and so much more. This book is a tool for learning and becoming proficient in the craft of drag racing. What this book does not provide is information for selecting a drag-racing car to suit your needs. Many magazines and websites cover the information and perspectives, so budding drag racers can make informed buying decisions.

My goal is to help you reach the winner's circle, and this book tries to help you do just that. More important, I want you to have fun because drag racing is a fantastic sport and it's filled with some of the most

incredible people you'll ever have the privilege to meet.

Because I have worked for *National DRAGSTER*, published by the National Hot Rod Association (NHRA) for 19 years, and have raced almost exclusively at NHRA events, I have focused on NHRA drag racing in this book. NHRA is a major sanctioning body for drag racing in the United States, and has a network of approximately 140 member tracks. All references to the NHRA Rulebook are to the 2008 edition.

Good luck, be safe, and we'll see you at the finish line.

NOTICE:

With NHRA's permission, I have set forth the warnings and admonitions NHRA gives to all those who participate in the sport of drag racing. It is important for you to read and understand this notice since it sets forth your important obligations as a participant in the sport:

Drag racing is a dangerous sport. There is no such thing as a guaranteed safe drag race. Drag racing always carries with it the risk of serious injury or death in any number of ways. This risk will always exist no matter how much everyone connected with drag racing

tries to make our sport safer. Although NHRA works to promote and enhance the safety of the sport, there are no guarantees that such safety measures will guarantee or ensure safety. A participant always has the responsibility for the participant's own safety, and by participating in drag racing, the participant accepts all risk of injury, whether due to negligence, vehicle failure, or otherwise. If at any time you do not accept these risks, you should not participate in drag racing.

Prime responsibility for the safe condition and operation of a vehicle in competition rests with the vehicle owner, driver, and crewmembers. The track operator's main concern is to provide a place to conduct events. NHRA produces guidelines based on experience and circulates information to help perpetuate the sport. Close observance of the standards set forth in the NHRA Rulebook is required for all participants. However, drag racing is dangerous. Therefore, no express or implied warranty of safety is created from publication of or compliance with NHRA Rules or the NHRA Rulebook, nor does compliance with NHRA rules or anything set forth in the Rulebook guarantee against injury or death to participants, spectators or others.

DRAG RACING: A SPORT OF UNIVERSAL APPEAL

On the surface, drag racing seems like a simple sport, and indeed it is. By definition, a drag race is a timed acceleration contest featuring two motor vehicles on a long straight course, usually measuring either a quarter-mile or eighth-mile in length (with additional room for deceleration). Drag-racing facilities also utilize some form of timing system to determine which vehicle arrived at the finish line first and how long it took each of them to get there.

The basics of drag racing are simple, yet there are intricacies that make it a perpetual challenge, even to the experienced racer. To paraphrase a saying from the game of poker, "Drag racing takes only a few minutes to learn, but a lifetime to master."

Challenging, yes, but the true beauty of drag racing is that virtually anyone can compete. There are no age, race, or gender barriers. From weekly ET (elapsed time) bracket races that feature primarily street-driven cars and motorcycles to full-fledged professional competition in 330-mph Top Fuel dragsters and Funny Cars, there are classes to fit just about any individual taste, skill level, and budget. Due to its mass appeal and accessibility, drag racing is easily the world's No. 1 participant-based motorsport, with literally thousands of racers competing each week at drag strips across North America.

To further illustrate the point, most of us can only take a lap around Indianapolis Motor Speedway in a tour bus, but in drag racing, it's possible to compete on the same tracks as John Force, Tony Schumacher, Warren Johnson, and the rest of today's top drag-racing stars. In most cases, all that is required to compete on a local level is a valid state driver's license and a vehicle that conforms to a few basic safety requirements. With the introduction of half-scale dragsters and the NHRA (National Hot Rod Association) Jr. Drag Racing League in 1992, participants as young as 8 years old can also experience the thrill of drag racing. It is truly a sport for the masses.

The formation of organized drag racing helped move drag racing off the street and onto the track, providing a safer and more regulated venue. Drag racers could test their driving skills, push their cars to the limit, and enjoy the thrill of side-by-side competition in more controlled conditions.

In the Beginning...

In order to fully comprehend contemporary drag racing, it helps to first understand the origins of the sport. While it's entirely possible that a rudimentary form of drag racing dates back to the days of the Roman Empire and involved horses, gladiators, and chariots, the sport as we know it today was founded on dry lake beds, city streets, old air port landing strips, which were the preferred location, and even sandy beaches in the days following World War II.

The first dragsters were often little more than street cars with slightly modified engines and bodies stripped to reduce weight. Later, purpose-built cars were constructed featuring advanced alterations to improve performance and safety.

Born on back roads and dry lake beds in the years following World War II, drag racing began to flourish in the early 1960s when the National Hot Rod Association began holding national meets, like the Winternationals in Pomona, California. In fact, the first official NHRA race was held at Pomona in April 1953 in a parking-lot area of the Los Angeles County Fairgrounds.

By 1950, the sport began to take shape when C.J. "Pappy" Hart opened the first commercial drag strip on an abandoned airport in Santa Ana, California. A year later, former Hot Rod magazine editor Wally Parks formed the National Hot Rod Association, which helped legitimize the sport by creating safety rules and performance standards.

One question frequently asked is, "Where did the term drag racing come from?" It's a great question but the truth is, not even late NHRA founder Wally Parks, the man most often credited with the creation of modern drag racing, had a definitive answer. One widely held theory is that the term comes from street racers who used to race on the "main drag," which was the name often used to describe the main street in many small towns. Another possibility is that early street racers used to delay or drag out each gear change in an effort to improve the performance of the vehicles.

Given a chance to rewrite history, perhaps a better term to describe acceleration contests might have been sprint racing, since quarter-mile drag racing is a quick sprint to the finish. Obviously, that designation is already in use for a different class of race.

Current dragsters evolved from early drag-race vehicles, such as Dick Kraft's Bug. This roadster was pared down to its bare frame rails, engine, transmission, and four wheels. Hence, these drag racers were aptly named "rail jobs." Equipped with a Ford flathead V-8, Kraft's Bug reached 109.09 mph on September 24, 1950, at Southern California's Santa Ana Drags.

In 1954, NHRA founder Wally Parks organized the Drag Safari, a group of dedicated individuals who toured the country, helping car clubs and other groups organize local drag-racing events. Parks and his dedicated crew helped launch organized drag racing, which millions of fans enjoy today, and encouraged street racers to race on the track. Their motto was is "Dedicated to Safety."

In 1954, Parks organized the Drag Safari, which was a group of dedicated individuals who traveled the country in a Pontiac station wagon and a small tag-along trailer, helping local car clubs organize and promote drag-racing events. The Drag Safari, which later became known as the Safety Safari, performed a tremendous service by taking unsupervised acceleration contests off the city streets and moved them to temporary courses (usually abandoned airport runways), which were much safer venues.

The first national gathering of drag-racing competitors was staged in Great Bend, Kansas, in 1955. This was the forerunner of today's popular NHRA national events, which feature hundreds of professional and sportsman competitors, tens of thousands of spectators, and a worldwide television audience in the millions.

Today, more than 50 years after its inception, the National Hot Rod Association is the largest motorsports organization in the world with approximately 80,000 members, many of whom are active participants. The NHRA POWERade Drag Racing Series (soon to be known as the NHRA Full Throttle Drag Racing Series) has grown to 24 events that are located in nearly every major U.S. market, including Los Angeles, New York, Dallas, Chicago, Atlanta, Houston, and Las Vegas, and are telecast on ESPN2. NHRA's grassroots programs, including the popular 44-race Lucas Oil Drag Racing Series, the Summit E.T. Racing Series, and the O'Reilly Jr. Drag Racing League, attract thousands of competitors.

Keeping with Wally Parks' original philosophy, safety and technological improvements remain a top priority. Progressive changes will help NHRA continue to fulfill its leadership role in the motorsports world well into the future.

Whether you occasionally race your family street car in grudge-racing events at your local track, or race a Top Fuel dragster on the NHRA POWERade tour, it should be plainly obvious that drag racing is a sport meant for everyone to enjoy. At any drag racing event you're likely to find an eclectic mix of racers from all walks of life. Let's face it, there aren't too many sports where a housewife can face off against a fire fighter, but unlikely gatherings of this sort

The ultimate form of drag racing is Top Fuel. Cars, such as Tony Schumacher's U.S. Army Top Fuel car, can reach 330 mph and run the quarter-mile in less than 4.5 seconds. Like any professional athlete, Top Fuel drivers have built and honed their skills through years of competition. The difference between winning and losing at this level usually comes down to a few hundredths, if not thousandths, of a second.

happen frequently on a drag strip. Men and women, young and old, rich and poor make up the many thousands of racers who regularly compete on the nation's drag strips. And they are not identifiable by a singular trait. However, they do share their love for high-performance automobiles and their strong desire to experience the thrill of competition.

Drag racing is also one of the few sports where men and women compete as equals. There are no powder puff races that are exclusive to female racers or ladies' trees to help equalize the competition. Women do not ask for, nor do they receive, any concessions from their male counterparts. Since the early 1960s, when racers such as Barbara Hamilton, Shirley Muldowney, Judy Lilly, and Paula Murphy began to break down gender barriers in motorsports, nearly 50 women have gone on to win an NHRA national event title. The women who have won local bracket-racing events probably number in the thousands, and women continue to make up one of drag racing's fastest-rising demographic groups. It's very obvious that female racers are not a novelty and haven't been for many, many years.

Drag racing is very much an equal-opportunity sport. If you have the ability to competently control a motor vehicle, accept the risks of the sport, and you are willing to race within your means mentally, financially, and otherwise, then you can not only compete, but you also have a reasonable chance to succeed. If you truly have a passion for racing, you'll never be made to feel like an outsider.

Much of drag racing's universal appeal stems from the fact that it is a true family sport. It is not uncommon to see second-, third-, or even fourth-generation racers.

How Far Can I Go?

You've decided to race; now it's time for you to determine which class best suits you. More often than not, the biggest factor in determining the best place for you to race will be your budget, but that isn't the only determining factor. You've also got to take into consideration your mechanical skills or those of your crew, the amount of time you're willing to devote to your racing operation, and perhaps most important, your emotional stake in what

In order to participate in most of the current street-legal programs, a driver needs the proper safety equipment and a valid state driver's license. It's a great introductory class for the novice driver to sample the sport, learn how to race, and decide whether to step up to a higher level of competition.

In an effort to combat the problem of illegal street racing, most tracks have a program specifically designed for street legal vehicles. Hence, there is a class for nearly every car, so almost any driver can "run what you brung."

shows. A professional racer's duties also include television, radio, and newspaper interviews, photo sessions, and face-to-face meetings with corporate executives. Therefore, the ability to speak well in front of a camera or a large group of people and the ability to maintain a professional appearance is just as important as driving the race car. Some of the sport's best-known drivers might spend just a few minutes at each event actually strapped into the cockpit of their racer car, but they rarely have a free moment to themselves because of all the other duties that go along with their chosen profession.

Technically, the term "professional racer" applies to anyone who earns money racing, but in most cases, it refers to those who compete in professional eliminators, such as Top Fuel, Funny Car, Pro Stock, and Pro Stock Motorcycle. However, there are some sportsman drivers who are able to race for a living, thus fitting the definition of a professional racer. Most of these drivers

you're doing. Determining your skill level should be simple. If you're capable of doing most of the work on your car or you have surrounded yourself with a number of competent people to help you, then you're likely to progress as far up the ladder as your budget will allow you to go.

In drag racing's formative years a hired driver was something of a rarity, as most team owners not only worked on their cars, but also enjoyed the benefits of driving them. Today, that isn't always the case as there are a large number of hired drivers in both professional and sportsman-class racing. So how does one become a hired driver? There is no universal answer to this question, but there are some general guidelines that any would-be driver should be willing to follow.

Obviously, a hired driver should have the ability to safely handle the vehicle, the nerve to face the dangers of high-speed racing, and, naturally, the talent to win rounds. Most hired

drivers active in racing today also have the added responsibility of representing their team owners and their sponsors, which often means that their duties also include numerous personal appearances at autograph signings, conventions, and trade

The introduction of the NHRA O'Reilly Auto Parts Jr. Drag Racing League in 1992 allowed kids as young as eight years old to experience the thrill and excitement of drag racing. Today, there are thousands of Jr. Drag racers across the country.

either win enough races that they're able to support themselves via the prize money they've won, or they've marketed themselves wisely and have acquired corporate sponsors to underwrite the cost of racing.

Technically, the term "professional racer" applies to anyone who earns money racing, but in most cases, it refers to those who compete in professional eliminators, such as Top Fuel, Funny Car, Pro Stock, and Pro Stock Motorcycle. However, there are some sportsman drivers who are able to race for a living, thus fitting the definition of a professional racer. Most of these drivers either win enough races that they're able to support themselves via the prize money they've won, or they've marketed themselves wisely and have acquired corporate sponsors to underwrite the cost of racing.

Time is also a critical factor when determining what type of vehicle to race and which class to compete in. Most bracket cars require a minimal amount of maintenance from week to week, which makes them perfect for an individual

Most of today's professional racers have duties that extend far beyond driving the race car. Autograph signings, trade shows, media appearances, and sponsor appearances are often a large part of a sponsorship program.

In many communities, the Beat the Heat program is an effective way to combat illegal street racing. With the Beat the Heat, racers have the opportunity to race against a modified police cruiser. This is yet another innovative program that encourages participation on the track and helps discourage street racing.

From a Stock eliminator car to a 300+-mph nitro-burning Funny Car, drag racing has a place to race for just about everyone. While your choices are virtually unlimited, your budget often determines how fast you'll ultimately go. For most newcomers, a bracket-racing class is the best place to start.

who works a regular job or otherwise has family or other commitments. In most cases, you can simply park the car after each event, perform a few routine safety checks and/or other maintenance-related duties during the week, and be ready to go racing again whenever you're so inclined. On the other hand, some other popular racing vehicles, particularly the quicker ones such as Top Alcohol Dragster, Top Alcohol Funny Cars, or Pro Mod cars, are much more labor intensive and require many hours of preparation and maintenance both in the garage and at the track. Again, it's up to the individual to decide which vehicle best suits his or her particular situation.

Finally, the important role that emotion plays in racing is too significant to overlook, especially when it comes to selecting which car to race or which class to compete in. To put it in simple terms, some racers are better equipped than others to deal with the various stresses and risks that inherently come with drag racing at its highest levels. It might sur-

The infrared photocell timing system works by projecting an invisible beam of light across the track, where it hits a reflector and then bounces back. When the infrared light beam is broken, the clocks are stopped.

prise you to know that there are some racers who regularly compete in bracket races or in NHRA sportsman classes that have the financial wherewithal, the driving ability, and the time necessary to compete in professional eliminators if they choose to do so. However, many of these racers aren't willing to make that leap because they realize that in order to succeed at that level, they've got to be equipped to deal with the highs and lows better than the average weekend warrior. In most cases, a professional race team is run as a business. In order to be successful,

By the early 1960s, photocells were used to time drag races with a reasonable degree of accuracy. Note that even as early as 1963 drag races were being filmed for television. Photocell timing legitimized the sport and made results much more reliable and accurate.

The Chrondek timing system, a staple of the industry for many years, used a pair of small digital readouts to record ETs and speeds for each lane.

the business usually requires constant attention, and the right mix of dedicated employees and competent leadership. Some of drag racing's biggest teams look more like mid-size companies than race teams and have as many as 20 to 30 or more full-time employees on the payroll.

Becoming a professional drag racer isn't much different from becoming a professional baseball or football player. Many aspire to get there, but the reality is that few actually make it. If you're willing and able to tackle that sort of a commitment, then there's a place for you at the sport's highest levels, but there is also a place for just about everyone else as well.

In a perfect world, race cars and all of the equipment necessary to race them would be cheap and plentiful, but unfortunately that isn't the case and it never has been. The old and often-used adage, "Speed costs. How fast do you want to go?" still rings true today, perhaps more now than ever. How much you can afford to spend on your racing operation is entirely up to you. If you've over-extended yourself in order to go racing, you'll probably be so worried about your finances that you won't be very competitive, and you almost certainly won't enjoy yourself. In turn, it's in your best interests to set a reasonable budget and have the discipline to stick to it.

The Basics

The Timing System

Some of the earliest organized drag races featured timing systems that were crude and often inaccurate. Some of the most primitive systems even used air hoses similar to the ones found in old gas stations, only instead of ringing a bell when the hose was run over, these ancient systems would start and stop the clocks using air pressure.

Today's timing systems feature the latest digital and fiber-optic technology in order to time each race accurately. As such, they have the ability to measure ETs (elapsed times) down to the one-millionth (0.000001) of a second. There are no ties in drag racing; each contest features a definitive winner, even if it isn't apparent to the naked eye.

Modern timing systems use a series of photocells located at

The reflectors that are placed along the centerline of the track are nothing more than foam blocks. Older timing systems used glass lamps, but errant drivers occasionally hit the lamps, causing a potentially serious problem and a lengthy cleanup. The foam blocks are held to the track with adhesive and are easily replaced in the event of an incident.

Unlike the old Chrondek clocks, the current timing systems, such as this one from Compulink, use a video monitor. The Compulink system not only times each race, but it provides elapsed times at 60 feet, 330 feet, 660 feet (eighth-mile), 1,000 feet, and 1,320 feet, which are recorded down to 0.001 second.

strategic points on the race track to calculate reaction time, ET, and speed. Each photocell shoots an invisible beam of infrared light across the track, where it hits a reflector mounted in the middle of each lane. The photocells are programmed to start and stop the timer whenever a vehicle's front tires interrupt the light beams. A computer monitor, located in the timing tower, provides a display of all pertinent information. For the fans in the stands, scoreboards post each driver's ET and speed.

It is important to note that each lane is individually timed and that the clocks do not start when the light turns green. The clocks actually start when the car moves out of the starting line stage beam. This part of the sport is often misunderstood by novice racers, but should be easy to comprehend after just one visit to the drag strip.

On most quarter-mile drag strips, ETs are recorded at the following increments: 60 feet, 330 feet, 660 feet (eighth-mile), 1,000 feet, and 1,320 feet. In addition, speed readings are taken at half-track and at the finish line. Many tracks race on an eighth-mile course, which obviously eliminates the need for 1,000-foot and 1,320-foot ETs. The timing system also records reaction time, which is the time between when the light on the Christmas tree turns green and the vehicle leaves the starting line. Reaction time, one of the most important elements for any successful racer, will be a central focus of this book and will be covered in depth in future chapters.

The Christmas Tree

In drag racing's formative years, drag races were started using

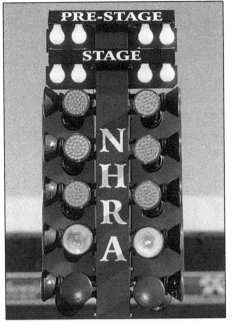

For many years, the Christmas-tree starting system featured five amber lights, which counted down at half-second intervals. This older-style tree does not have pre-stage lights, just one set of stage bulbs to indicate that each driver is ready to race.

The Christmas tree that is used today features bright LED bulbs, and is visible from the front, back, and sides. Though they aren't all visible in this photo, the modern Christmas tree features 46 light bulbs. A car's wheels first break the beam to pre-stage and then the car inches forward to break the second set of beams to trigger the stage light.

Now a part of drag-racing lore, a flagman signaled the start of drag races until the introduction of the Christmas tree in 1963. By anticipating the flagman's first move, some highly skilled drivers were able to gain an edge on their competitors. Hence, the Christmas tree helped level the playing field.

a flagman, who would stand in the center of the race track and give each driver the signal to go by waving a pair of flags. The flagman also acted as a referee, using his judgment to determine if a competitor jumped the start before the flag had waved. As one might imagine, just like in traditional stick-and-ball sports, the human element of the flagman was often imperfect, and disputes between competitors were common.

The beginning of the end for the flagman came at the 1963 NHRA Nationals at Indianapolis, where the first "Christmas tree" starting system was introduced. An article that ran in the July 26, 1963, issue of NHRA's National DRAGSTER magazine noted that the new starting system, deemed the "electronic flagger," would be "foolproof in design" and "will be a boon to nervous young drivers trying for the big win."

Despite the optimistic forecast, the first Christmas tree, like many other radical innovations, was initially met with some resistance, particularly from those drivers who were adept at anticipating the movements of the flagman, and were able to use that information to gain an advantage over their competitors. However, there is no denying that the Christmas tree achieved its primary goal, which was to assure a fair start for all competitors, and more than 40 years later, the flagman has gone the way of the Edsel and the black-and-white television.

The modern Christmas tree is fairly easy to understand. As a competitor rolls forward towards the starting line, the infrared beam will detect the vehicle's front wheel, activating the top yellow light, which is called the pre-stage light. The pre-stage light serves no other purpose than to let the driver know that he is approximately 6 to 8 inches from the starting line. At this point, most drivers make any last-second adjustments, and are fully prepared to race before moving forward into the stage beam.

Slowly rolling forward, the driver will activate the stage light, which is an indication that he or she is ready to race. When both competitors have illuminated the stage light, the starter will throw a switch that activates the Christmas tree starting system. In most forms of racing, particularly ET-bracket events, the three amber lights in the middle of the Christmas tree will count down one by one, at half-second intervals. This is known as a "Sportsman" or "full tree."

Other forms of drag racing use what is known as a "pro start," or

Drag Strip Timing and Scoring System Configuration

1. PRE-STAGED BEAM:
An infrared beam sender/receiver connection (per lane) triggers pre-staged lights and signals drivers that they are close to "staging" when this beam is broken by vehicle's front wheel.

2. STAGED BEAM/STARTING LINE:
This infrared beam sender/receiver connection controls the starting and timing of each race. This beam triggers an independent "lane timer" for elapsed time and will trigger the red foul light if a false start occurs. A race cannot be started until both competitors are fully "staged." The staged beam is located seven inches past the pre-staged beam.

3. INTERVAL TIMERS:
Time and speed are recorded at five intervals along the track. There are clocking devices at the 60-, 330-, 660-, 1,000-foot, and 1/4-mile (finish line) locations.

4. SPEED TRAPS AND ELAPSED-TIME CLOCK BEAMS:
The first infrared beam sender/receiver trigger marks the beginning of the speed trap and is located 66 feet before the finish line. It is used to start the individual lane top speed clocks. A second beam, which is located at the finish line and serves as the end of the speed trap, shuts off both the individual lane elapsed-time and top speed clocks, and triggers the win-light indicator in the deserving lane.

The length of the actual racing surface at an NHRA Drag Racing Series event is one-quarter mile, or 1,320 feet. The average width of each lane is 30 feet.

The following chart illustrates the layout of a contemporary drag strip, which includes pits, tech inspection, and the track. It also provides some insight into how timing and scoring works for each race. (Courtesy of the NHRA)

"pro tree," in which all three amber lights come on at once. On a pro tree, the interval between the amber lights and the green light can be either 4/10 second (.400) or 5/10 (.500) depending on class that is being contested or individual track rules. Once again, it is important to note that the clocks do not start until the vehicle's front tires move completely out of the stage beam. If the vehicle clears the stage beam before the light turns green, that is considered a foul start and the red light will illuminate. A foul start is grounds for disqualification.

Early versions of the Christmas tree featured five yellow lights, meaning that a driver had to wait 2.5

Drivers preparing to race gather in the staging lanes, where vehicles in similar classes are normally grouped together. By the time a vehicle enters the staging lanes, driver and car should be fully prepared to race. A track official will direct you to pull your car forward when the time comes. Once you've been paired up, put on your helmet and secure your seat belts in preparation for racing.

seconds between the first amber light and the green light before mashing the throttle. By the mid-1980s, the five-amber Christmas tree was replaced by a shorter version that featured just three amber lights and reduced the time a driver had to wait by a full second.

The most recent incarnation of the Christmas tree was introduced in 2003, and LED lights replaced the standard incandescent lights. The extra brightness of the LED lights helped driver reaction times by as much as 0.03-0.04 second. The current Christmas tree used at NHRA national events features a whopping total of 46 lights that are visible not only from the front, but also the back and the sides. The lights on the back and sides do not affect the driver and are largely there so that fans can see the tree from virtually any angle.

Track Layout

While the layout of each drag strip varies from track to track, most

have similar characteristics and feature several distinctive geographic areas, each one with its own purpose. You should always check out the whole facility and make sure you are comfortable racing there. You should walk the track to become familiar with the layout and to make sure everything is to your satisfaction. If you are not satisfied with the track, contact a track official, and if you are still not satisfied, you should not race. Check out the track from end-to-end to satisfy yourself that this is a suitable place to race. The following is a quick review of some important locations at the drag strip.

Pit area: If you are a participant, after you pay your entry fee, sign the Release & Waiver Agreement, and pass through the front gate, and your vehicle passes a technical inspection, you will be directed to the pit area where you may park for the duration of the event. On most race days, the pit area will be filled with race cars, trucks, trailers, motor homes, and other support equipment. Since most

The burnout area is located just behind the starting line. In this area, drivers roll though a puddle of water in an area called the water box, burnout box and spin their tires. A correctly executed burnout lays down a thin layer of hot rubber on the track surface and cleans as well as heats up the tires in order to gain maximum traction on the starting line.

races last only a few seconds, competitors will spend most of their time in the pit area. As such, most maintenance, preparation, and repair work is also performed here.

Staging lanes: From the pit area, competitors make their way to the starting line via several numbered lanes known as staging lanes. Com-petitors are usually called to the staging lanes in groups, with vehicles in the same class sharing the same lanes. By the time a vehicle reaches the staging lanes, car and driver should be fully prepared to race, since at this point, there is often only time for last-minute items such as a quick check of tire pressure. Likewise, drivers should also be organized and prepared when they reach the staging lanes. When called to staging, the drivers need to bring their run card or other form of registration. In particular, they should have all of the safety equipment in place before moving forward to make a run. Typically, the run card is shown to the track official at the back of the lanes, so he or she can verify that the entry fee has been paid. At most tracks, the official will direct drivers to a lane. At the front of the line, an official may ask for the card and punch it, so the upcoming run is recorded on the run card.

Burnout box: The burnout area, sometimes known as a water box, is located just behind the starting line and features an area where drivers can spin their tires in a puddle of water, heating them in a ritual that is known as a burnout. The purpose of a burnout is twofold. First, a good burnout cleans tires of any debris and heats them to a proper operating temperature. A burnout also puts down a thin layer of hot rubber on the track surface, which helps the vehicle gain traction on the starting line. Later in the book there will be an entire chapter devoted to tires and proper burnout techniques.

The driver heats the tires by performing a burnout in the water box, which is located several feet behind the starting line. You'll want to roll completely through the water before beginning your burnout. Avoid a rookie mistake and do not start your burnout in the water.

Starting line: Rolling out of the burnout box, drivers slowly make their way to the starting line to begin the careful staging process. Prior to activating the pre-stage light, most drivers will take a few seconds to collect their thoughts, and make a final check of engine-temperature and oil-pressure gauges. Once the staging process has begun, a driver's attention should be focused on the Christmas tree and all crewmembers should be clear of the vehicle.

Drag strip and finish line: After leaving the starting line, a driver

At the end of each run, you'll get a time slip, which is essentially a report card of your and your car's performance. Most time slips include a wealth of information including reaction time, ET, top speed, and margin of victory for the winner.

At most drag strips, a large scoreboard displays important information for each driver and the fans in the stands, including dial-ins, elapsed times, and speeds. In this instance, a dial-in of 9.45 seconds is displayed.

This is the view a driver gets when approaching the starting line. At this point, the driver must be focused on properly staging and launching the car. Once off the line, the driver keeps the car straight, accurately shifts, and prepares to shut down on reaching the finish line.

should focus on keeping the car straight and under control, hitting shift points at appropriate times, and preparing to shut down once reaching the finish line. At most tracks, the finish line is clearly marked by a stripe painted across the track and sometimes on the guard walls that line each lane. The scoreboards will usually be located at the finish line, though that is not the case with every track. In order to be sure, it alway pays to check out the finish line prior to making a run. Many tracks also have a light on the guard wall just past the finish line, which will indicate which driver won the race. Obviously, a light on in your lane is a very welcome sight.

Shutdown area: At the conclusion of a run, a driver's attention should shift to getting the vehicle slowed to a safe speed. The length of a shutdown area can vary from track to track, but most racers, especially those driving a street car, should have no problems bringing their car to a safe stop after a run. In the rare event that a driver has a brake failure or can't get his or her vehicle stopped for some other reason, most tracks have features at the end of the shutdown area that are designed to help arrest a runaway vehicle. These can include sand or gravel traps, catch nets, barrels, or unpaved areas. Still, no system is foolproof and no track is unlimited in length. It remains at all times the driver's obligation to slow the car and keep it under control if accidents are to be avoided.

In the shutdown area, it is also important to have an awareness of where your competitor is since you will likely both be using the same exit from the shutdown area and onto the return road. Depending on which side of the track the return road is located, one racer will have to cross the centerline of the track in order to exit the racing surface.

Return road: The return road is used to lead drivers back into the pit area at the conclusion of a run. On the return road, you will also find an ET shack or booth, where you will receive a time slip, which is essentially a report card of your run, listing such pertinent data as reaction time, ETs at various points on the track and, most important, whether you won or lost the race.

Types of Drag Racing

ET Bracket Racing

Whoever said that "variety is the spice of life" was probably a drag racer because no matter what type of vehicle you fancy, chances are you can find a place to race it on a drag strip.

In drag racing's formative years, the sport was simple to understand. The first driver to the finish line was declared the winner and the driver with the fastest car was usually the one who carried home the most trophies. However, as the sport grew and vehicles became more sophisticated (and expensive), race-track operators began looking for new and innovative ways to level the playing field for all competitors. The need for cost control and fair competition led to the creation of ET bracket racing.

ET bracket racing is the most basic and by far the most popular form of drag racing. Often simply referred to as bracket racing, it is a form of competition where vehicles are handicapped according to their performance. In other words, a slower car is given a head start over a faster one.

In bracket racing, competitors have the ability to choose their own dial-in, which is essentially an estimation or prediction of their vehicle's performance. Each individual race is handicapped according to each competitor's dial-in. Put simply, a racer who has chosen a dial-in of 12.00 seconds will receive a 2-seconds head start over an opponent with a dial-in of 10.00 seconds. A clock operator, who sits in the timing tower, programs each racer's dial-in time into the timing system. In a handicap race, one side of the Christmas tree will start before the other, giving the slower driver the necessary head start needed to make a fair race. Incidentally, dial-ins are normally written on the side and rear windows in ordinary shoe polish, so the tower personnel can easily see them.

Of course, a handicap start isn't enough to guarantee a fair race. A competitor could gain an advantage using a practice known as sandbagging, which is simply selecting a dial-in that does not reflect his or her vehicle's true performance potential. In order to prevent this practice, the easiest and most effective solution to the problem was the introduction of the breakout rule, which puts the emphasis on driver skill and vehicle consistency rather than all-out performance.

A breakout occurs when a driver runs quicker than his dial-in. In bracket racing, a driver who breaks out loses the race, even though he may have gotten to the finish line ahead of his opponent. If both drivers happen to break out (which is a fairly common occurrence), then the driver who is under his dial-in by the least amount is declared the winner. Because of the breakout rule, it is common to see bracket racers lift off the throttle or even tap the brake pedal before the finish line if they feel they are well ahead of their opponent. It is also common to see a bracket race that is so close that the naked eye is unable to determine a winner, but the electronic photocells at the finish line are always able to determine a winner because there are no ties in drag racing.

In addition to choosing the correct dial-in and avoiding a breakout, the other key to success in bracket racing is reaction time, which is a measure of a driver's reflexes on the starting line. Reaction time will be covered in depth in future chapters, but as a quick introduction, reaction time is the time between when the light on the Christmas tree turns green and the vehicle actually leaves the starting line. At the risk of oversimplifying the process, most drivers try to step on the gas as soon as the bottom yellow light flashes. There

Once you reach the finish line, the scoreboard will display your ET in the top panel and your top-end speed on the lower panel. The lights at the very top of the scoreboard indicate the race winner.

ET bracket racing is one of the most popular forms of motorsports competition in North America. Using a handicap-start system, bracket competition makes it possible for vehicles of differing performance levels to compete on an even playing field. Bracket racing requires competitors to set a target time or dial-in time for the quarter-mile. The driver that crosses the finish line closest to his or her dial-in time wins the race. This type of racing contains costs, puts a premium on driver skill, and rewards consistency.

While they might resemble ET bracket cars, Super Stock cars are much more technologically advanced. In Super Stock and Stock, there is a seemingly endless set of rules that severely limit engine and body modifications and govern nearly everything else from tire size to weight.

One of the most popular classes in all of drag racing is Super Comp. In this class, which is inhabited primarily by dragsters, there are no handicap starts. Instead, drivers shoot for a common 8.90-second index. There are also classes that use 7.90-, 9.90-, and 10.90- second indexes. If a driver is under these index times, the driver has broken out and is disqualified.

are many factors that influence reaction time, including vehicle performance, tire size, gearing, and driver ability. Most successful bracket racers have the ability to adjust their reaction times to account for a number of variables, and it is common for a good racer to leave the starting line just a few thousandths of a second after the green light comes on.

As noted earlier, bracket racing puts a premium on driver skill. An unlimited budget may allow a racer to build a fast race car, which is highly modified and extremely detailed, but this isn't necessarily an advantage. According to the rules of bracket racing, a street-legal economy car, such as a Toyota Celica, that might run the quarter-mile in 17 seconds or more, has a chance to successfully compete against a highly modified race car like a dragster that might run in the 8-second range. The ability to post good reac-

tion times and make consistent runs is the key to success in bracket racing. The ability to neutralize the advantage of someone who has an excess of wealth or mechanical ability is what makes bracket racing so popular. Most drag strips have a variety of bracket-racing classes, and most of them are designed to allow cars of similar performance levels to race against each other. This means that, in most cases, racers who choose to drive their street cars are likely to be racing against other street cars and not race-only cars.

While some may view bracket racing as an amateur form of competition, aimed primarily at beginner or novice racers, that is far from the truth. Many tracks across the country host large bracket-racing events, and these attract hundreds of competitors who race for large sums of money. It is common for a skilled bracket racer to win $10,000

or more during a single event, and there are a select few who possess the skills to carve out a successful living as professional bracket racers, with prize money as their sole source of revenue.

The NHRA also crowns world champions of bracket racing each year as part of its successful Summit ET Series, a multi-tiered program in which the winners of local and regional events earn the right to compete in a winner-take-all championship round that is held annually in Pomona, California. So while bracket racing may be the best way for newbies to get acquainted with the sport, it also presents a variety of opportunities for the more seasoned competitor.

Competition Eliminator, Super Stock, and Stock Class Racing

While bracket racing is extremely popular, and has been for

The official NHRA Rulebook offers literally hundreds of different classes, which should suit almost anyone's individual taste or budget. This Subaru-powered dragster is a competitive entry in Comp Eliminator.

Drag racing is one of the few sports where men and women compete as equals. There are no limitations when it comes to age, race, or gender. You need the appropriate launching and car-control skills, as well as the ability to be calm under pressure, but success is determined by how you drive, not by who you are.

the better part of four decades, there are many racers who still prefer to devote their efforts to improving the performance of their vehicle, rather than focusing solely on improving consistency. For those racers who enjoy all-out performance and don't mind working within the confines of strict rules, NHRA classes such as Competition Eliminator, Super Stock, and Stock might be to their liking.

Large sections of the official NHRA Rulebook are devoted to the rules and regulations that govern Comp, Super Stock, and Stock. These include limitations on everything from engine size and vehicle weight, to tire selection and fuel type. Comp, Super Stock, or Stock vehicles are very sophisticated race cars and feature vast amounts of technology.

Super Stock and Stock races follow a format that is similar to bracket racing. The main difference is that when two vehicles are in the same class, the race is an all-out battle to the finish line with no breakout rule in effect. There are more than 100 classes in Comp, Super Stock, and Stock, and each class is assigned an index, which represents what a well-built, well-prepared vehicle should run. Similar to bracket racing, the index is used to level the playing field and handicap vehicles of different performance levels. The breakout rule is not used in Comp, although the class does use a complex system known as the Competition Index

Control (CIC), which automatically adjusts the index for competitors who run too quickly.

Super Classes

Super-class racing, a variation of bracket racing, is the next logical step up the ladder for many aspiring racers. The main difference between bracket racing and Super-class racing is that competitors in the Super classes no longer have the option of choosing their own dial-in. A fixed index, usually 8.90, 9.90, or 10.90 seconds, replaces the dial-in. As in bracket racing, running under the index is a breakout and is not permitted.

In NHRA competition, the Super classes are Super Comp (8.90), Super Gas (9.90), and Super Street (10.90). Some areas also have classes for competitors running on a fixed 7.90-second index. The Super Comp class is populated almost exclusively by rear-engined dragsters, though roadsters and full-bodied "door slammer" cars are also permitted. Dragsters are not permitted in Super Gas or Super Street, and roadsters must be of the left-hand drive variety in order to compete in those two "eliminators" (all of more than 200 NHRA-governed classes of race vehicles are grouped into 12 categories, or eliminators).

Another difference between bracket racing and Super-class racing is the Christmas tree starting system. Almost all Bracket races use the full tree or "five-tenths" tree, which uses a countdown sequence of three lights at half-second intervals. Super-class racers use a pro tree, so named because it is the same starting system as professional competitors use. With a pro tree, all three yellow lights flash simultaneously, and there is just 4/10 second between the yellow lights and the green light. The exception is super street, which uses a 5/10 pro tree.

Once again, driver skill is paramount to success in Super-class racing. As in bracket competition, Super-class drivers must drive "both ends" of the race track, which means they must not only concentrate on a good reaction time on the starting line, but they must also "drive the finish line." This means they try to win the race by the narrowest margin possible, which reduces the odds of a breakout. It is common for bracket and Super-class racers to employ a strategy of allowing an opponent to cross the finish line first, if they believe they're going to break out.

Professional Racing

For those who possess an insatiable need for speed, the epitome of drag-racing competition is the professional classes, including Top Fuel dragsters, Funny Cars, Pro Stock cars, and Pro Stock motorcycles. This is the kind of drag racing that is most familiar to fans, since professional races are most often covered on television and in newspapers. NASCAR and Indy Car events may be exciting, but drag racing is unique since it is the only land-based motorsport in which competitors regularly exceed 300 mph. Fans who attend major drag-racing events also have the unique opportunity to meet their favorite drivers since they are allowed into the pit area for an up-close and personal view of the action.

Make no mistake, racing in any professional class requires a huge investment of time and money. It is common for today's top pro teams to have more than 20 full-time employees, several tractor trailer rigs to haul their equipment to and from each event, and an annual operating budget of $2–$3 million or more, which is often subsidized by a major corporate sponsor. The fortunate few who are hired to be professional drag-race drivers have usually spent years honing their skills while racing in slower classes. Years ago, a driver who displayed natural driving ability could often expect to become a hired driver, but with the advent of corporate sponsors, today's pro racers must be as comfortable standing in front of a television camera as they are sitting behind a butterfly steering wheel.

There are other drag-racing classes, including Top Alcohol Dragster and Top Alcohol Funny Car, which can provide a stepping-stone into the pro ranks. These are not technically professional classes, but they require a substantial investment of time, money, and labor.

Admittedly, racing at 330 mph, spending months on the road, and pitching products for a major sponsor isn't for everyone. As this book will illustrate, though, drag racing doesn't need to be done at a professional level to be fun, profitable, and rewarding.

Funny Car teams typically have a crew of a dozen people or more, including a crew chief, mechanics, and other personnel, and an annual budget of $3 million or more. John Force (pictured), the most successful Funny Car driver in the history of the sport, prepares for a run.

A League of Their Own

The majority of today's baseball and football heroes began their careers early, acquiring their skills as youngsters in local Little League or Pop Warner leagues. Likewise, many successful NASCAR and open-wheel racers began their careers racing karts or quarter-midgets many years before they were old enough to get a driver's license. Drag racing had no such feeder system until the late Vinny Napp, the founder and track manager of Old Bridge Township Raceway Park in Englishtown, New Jersey, created what is now known as the Jr. Drag Racing League.

Throughout his career, Napp was a visionary, but when he built the first Jr. Dragster in 1991, he wasn't planning on creating a national phenomenon—he simply wanted his young children to be able to experience the thrill of drag racing. The first Jr. Dragster was essentially a half-scale version of a modern Super Comp dragster, complete with a roll cage and a butterfly steering wheel. The car was powered by a 5-hp, single-cylinder Briggs & Stratton engine. Racing on an eighth-mile course, the dragster ran 12-second elapsed times at close to 50 mph.

The first Jr. Dragster was officially unveiled on July 9, 1992, during the 23rd annual Mopar Parts Nationals in Englishtown. An exhibition race featuring Napp's son, David, and Jill Caliendo was run. Just two years later, NHRA sponsored the first Jr. Drag Racing League National Championships at O'Reilly Raceway Park in Indianapolis, Indiana, which drew more than 500 young drivers. Napp may not have planned it this way, but today, more than 4,500 members compete in the O'Reilly Auto Parts NHRA Jr. Drag Racing League, and it has become a breeding ground for many of the sport's future champions. NHRA Jr. Drag Racing events are regularly held at many NHRA Member Tracks. Each summer, NHRA hosts an Eastern Conference Finals race in Bristol, Tennessee, and a Western Conference Finals in Denver, Colorado, where participants from 8 to 18 years old compete for trophies and more than $100,000 in savings bonds.

The true spirit of hot rodding is alive and well in the NHRA Jr. Drag Racing League. Many as there are many manufacturers who offer an endless array of "go-fast" parts just for Jr. Dragsters, including special clutches, cylinder heads, carburetors, and ignitions. It is not uncommon for today's Jr. Dragsters to cover the eighth -mile in less than 8 seconds at speeds approaching 85 mph. In fact, NHRA has placed speed and elapsed time restrictions on competitors based on their age and experience.

A state-of-the-art Jr. Dragster with custom paint, lots of chrome, and all of the latest performance upgrades can run upwards of $12,000 to $15,000. However, it is still possible for budget-minded families to get involved in the sport for less than half of that amount.

Not surprisingly, many of today's young drag racing stars began their careers racing in the Jr. Drag Racing League. These include Pro Stock racers Richie Stevens and Erica Enders, and Top Fuel driver J.R. Todd, who won the prestigious Automobile Club Road to the Future award as NHRA's top professional rookie in 2006. Many of young guns who are winning regularly in NHRA's sportsman classes have made literally thousands of runs in Jr. Dragster competition. Thus, they are very well prepared when they finally graduate to "real cars."

Enders, along with her younger sister, Courtney, may have done as much as anyone to help fuel the growth of Jr. Drag Racing. They were the subject of the 2003 Disney movie, Right on Track, which followed their exploits in the Jr. Drag Racing League.

NHRA Jr. Drag Racing League activities allow novices to learn the fundamentals of drag racing and have been the breeding ground for future drag racing champions.

HOW TO GET STARTED IN DRAG RACING

Like any new endeavor, a little research beforehand can go a long way toward making your first trip to the drag races a fun and rewarding experience. Most tracks now have their own website, so it's a good idea to start there when gathering information. A directory of NHRA member tracks is in Appendix D, and you can also log on to NHRA.com for a current listing and links to many track's websites. Most websites should be able to answer any questions you might have

regarding the track's schedule of events, admission cost, payout, class structure, and track rules, which sometimes vary greatly. For example, all tracks require drivers of vehicles running 13.99 seconds and quicker to wear a helmet, but some tracks require all drivers to wear helmets, so it's best to check first.

If you don't find the information online, you can always call the track with any questions you might have. At the very least, the track should

have a pre-recorded message that will tell you when the gates open and how much the admission fee is.

I've mentioned NHRA member tracks before, and it is important to recognize what these tracks are and what they are not. A "Member Track" is an independently owned and operated racing facility that has made an agreement with NHRA to run drag races at the facility under NHRA rules. I say "racing facility" because many of these places often offer more than drag racing. These racing facilities may also have oval tracks and road courses in addition to a drag strip. In order to become an NHRA Member Track, the drag racing facility must meet certain basic criteria and must otherwise be suitable for their desired level of drag racing. Their tech inspectors must be SFI certified and familiar with NHRA rules. A Member Track has permission to use the NHRA logo, but a Member Track and its own events always remain separate from NHRA. The NHRA does not "sanction" race tracks. It only sanctions NHRA events. The NHRA does not sanction a particular race at a Member Track unless it is hosting

One lane will sometimes provide better traction than the other. After running both lanes, you should determine which lane is quicker for you and run that lane as you progress through the rounds. However, as the track changes throughout the day, the slower lane may become the faster lane and it may switch again, so you need to be aware of the condition of the track.

No matter if you're building your own race car or buying one that is used, it's important that you fit comfortably inside the cockpit and that pedals, steering wheel, shifter, and all switches are within easy reach. If your car isn't comfortable, your performance will almost certainly suffer.

If you're racing a street car at a local bracket-racing event, you will be required to wear pants, proper shoes, and a helmet. Safety should never be taken lightly. And, you can always exceed the minimum safety requirements for your vehicle. When it comes to buying a helmet, a fire jacket, and other equipment, always select top-quality items. If you are involved in an accident or crash, its quality and protective capacity will pay off.

the event and NHRA officials are present. Otherwise, the race is strictly a Member Track event, which the NHRA does not conduct. Some

Before you arrive at the track, you should know which class or classes you will be running. If you are not certain of the class your car will run, then it is one of the decisions you will have to make. Most tracks have a trophy or beginner class that is perfect for first-time or novice racers. If you're not sure what class you should compete in, consult someone who is familiar with all the drag-racing classes.

A racer needs to follow a regular maintenance schedule, monitor performance, and keep his or her car properly tuned. You need to take the time to properly prepare, inspect, and maintain your race car before you head for the drag strip. If you have to deal with performance and reliability problems at the race track, you attention will be diverted from driving to mechanical issues, and this doesn't help the novice racer develop his or her race craft.

Member Tracks will have more than one NHRA event in a given racing season. Some tracks will have none. How will you know if the race is NHRA sanctioned or a Member Track event? NHRA events are advertised as such and are almost always part of a sponsored racing series. Almost all of the racing at Member Tracks will be their own events with their own officials using NHRA rules. If you're not sure, contact the NHRA divisional office in your area for a schedule of NHRA events.

After you've done your homework, you should have a basic understanding of how your local track operates. It's always a good idea to arrive as early as possible, so you'll have plenty of time to get settled and familiarize yourself with the layout of the track and the pit area. This is also a good time to meet your fellow racers. Even though you'll be competing against these people, most of them are more than willing to help. The camaraderie that exists among drag racers is second to none; more often than not, all you have to do is ask and someone will be willing to help you.

Before you head to the track, it's also a good idea to pack a few necessities because you're likely to be there for most of the day or night. Some of the things you want to bring along might include some basic hand tools, a tire-pressure gauge, an approved helmet, other safety gear required for your vehicle, sunscreen, shoe polish (for numbering your car), food and beverages.

One other thing that no racer should be without is a logbook, or at the very least a notebook, so you can begin to collect data on each event you attend and every run you make. In future chapters, we'll explain how good record keeping is an essential

It's best to arrive early at the race track so you can have a better chance of getting an ideal spot in the pit area. The pit areas usually are packed with cars, so don't hog space. Since this will be your base of operations for the event, a location close to the staging lanes is advantageous so that you are able to maximize work time on your car between rounds.

Track workers use a propane torch to prevent water being dragged from the burnout area to the starting line. The starting line official and track workers try to keep the starting line area dry and clean, for better race conditions.

part of any successful racer's program. With that in mind, it's best to start at the beginning so plan on taking some notes.

Most tracks and the NHRA Rulebook have a simple dress code, which requires all participants no matter what the speed of the vehicle to wear at minimum a short-sleeve shirt, long pants, and shoes (not sandals or flip flops) while racing. This might be stating the obvious, but a hat and a pair of sunglasses are also recommended.

Some tracks, particularly those that feature street-legal racing programs, might also require you to bring current vehicle registration and proof of insurance in order to compete. Also, if you are under 18 years of age, a parent or legal guardian needs to sign a parental consent form known as a Minor Release and Waiver, which you can obtain from NHRA.

Once you arrive at the track, the first order of business is to pay your entry fee. You'll also have to decide which class you're going to compete

in. It's possible and highly likely that your vehicle might even be suitable for more than one class, so you'll often have to make a decision.

In most cases, vehicles are classified according to ET so if you're racing in your daily driver, you'll most likely be in the slowest class, usually known as Sportsman or Street Eliminator.

If you're a first-timer, you probably should enter a trophy class because in all likelihood, you'll be racing against other first-timers. Another alternative is to just make time runs, which allows you to hone your driving and tuning skills before entering actual competition. For this purpose, most tracks have dedicated days for testing and tuning; they are also called Grudge Nights.

Once you gain a little experience and begin to feel comfortable, you can move into one of the more advanced classes in which you'll actually be racing for prize money. Some tracks will even allow beginners to simply make time-trial runs during the event. That way, you can

gauge the performance of your car without the added pressure of competing against other racers during eliminations.

Upon entering the track, you will also receive a technical inspection form, or "tech card," which is used by the track as a record of each competitor and his or her vehicle and as a record of the tech inspection. Remember to fill out the tech card completely and legibly since this card will also be used to provide information to the track announcer and possibly the track reporter or local newspaper. If the announcer mispronounces your name or hometown, chances are it is because your tech card wasn't filled out legibly.

Technical inspection assists event officials with determining, in their judgment, eligibility for participation in an event. Keep in mind, the technical inspection is not exhaustive and does not ensure that the vehicle or any part of it is safe. As a result, the technical inspection does not in any way change the fact that the driver, the crewmembers and the vehicle owner are ultimately responsible for the operation of the vehicle and equipment. Don't expect a tech inspector to find any or every problem your vehicle or safety gear might have; that is your responsibility.

You'll also be asked to sign a Release & Waiver Agreement before being allowed to compete. If you've never seen it before, read it carefully. It releases the track and everyone else from liability in the event of an accident. You are also agreeing to assume the risk of any injuries, since there are ever-present dangers in this sport. (See the form attached in the Appendices.)

Next, you should find a parking spot in the pit area, which will be your home base for the duration of the event. Normally, pit parking spaces are available on a first come, first served basis but at some places, the best spots (usually paved and well-lit) are reserved for racers competing in the quicker classes. Some facilities even sell their premier pit spots to their regular customers or award them as prizes to track champions.

After you've settled in your pit spot and unloaded your equipment, it's time to go through the tech inspection process, which is explained below. After your car has passed tech inspection, it's almost time to go racing. When the track announcer calls your class to the staging lanes, you'll have the opportunity to make a couple of practice runs, called time trials, before proceeding into final eliminations.

Track Personnel and Job Descriptions

Anytime you visit a drag strip, you can expect to encounter a group of hard-working and dedicated individuals who perform a variety of critical tasks that are necessary in order to provide a more controlled environment for racing, and to enforce rules aimed to provide fair competition for all. The following is a review of some of the more visible track workers and their job descriptions.

Before any vehicle can make a run down the drag strip, it must first pass a technical inspection. A valid state-issued driver's license, registration, and proof of insurance are also usually required.

Before each event, officials check each car, remembering that the driver has the ultimate responsibility to be sure his or her vehicle is ready to race. Here, NHRA Tech Officials check the body dimensions of a Top Alcohol Funny Car.

Tech Inspector

Every vehicle that participates in a drag-racing event must first pass a technical inspection. As noted earlier, most street cars can be raced with little or no modifications, so tech inspection should be brief and, in most cases, painless. Rules vary greatly from track to track, but at the very minimum, your vehicle must have good tread on the tires and all lug nuts must be in place and properly tightened. The brake pedal should also have a solid "feel." Most tracks will also require an overflow container for the radiator and, of course, properly installed seat belts. A Snell-rated helmet may also be required.

The tech inspector may also check for things like an exhaust system that isn't properly secured, broken or excessively cracked window glass, a battery that isn't properly tied down, and fluid leaks. It's also a good idea to make sure your car is clean before taking it to the track. Even if your car isn't a candidate for a "Best Appearing Car" award, it's important to have a clean car, so it shouldn't have mud or dirt caked onto the wheels, tires, or fender wells. Few things are more embarrassing than being backed off the starting line because you've spilled fluid or dumped dirt on the track surface.

For faster cars, additional safety equipment is often required, including a driveshaft loop, a roll bar or roll cage, and a safety harness and/or a window net. Bottom line: If your car isn't safe enough to drive on the street, it shouldn't be in competition on a drag strip. Also, it is your responsibility to make sure your car and gear are safe and meet all of the rules for your class. Don't just rely on the tech inspector to catch any potential problem with your car.

That's not his job—it's yours. All of the exact rules can be found in the NHRA Rulebook, which can be purchased for about $10. The rulebook also explains in great detail the race procedures and different racing classes run in the National Hot Rod Association. Note, however, that there are other sanctioning bodies, and there may be specific track rules not found in the rulebook.

Staging-Lane Director

Once you have gone through the technical inspection process and have completed the necessary preparation in order to make a run down the drag strip, the next individual you will encounter is the staging-lane director. The staging-lane director's primary duty is to direct traffic, and to make sure that each vehicle is in the proper lane and ready to race. In most cases, similar cars are classified together and will compete against each other. For instance, if you are entered in the Sportsman division, you will make your time-trial and elimination runs along with the rest of the competitors in that class. As a general rule, each class will use two staging lanes, the left lane for vehicles racing in the left lane and the right lane for competitors who favor the right lane. In most cases, you will have the option to choose either lane.

During time trial runs, it is generally a good idea to make at least one run in each lane because most tracks and drivers will have slight variances in reaction time and ET from lane to lane. Depending on where you're racing and what time of the day it is, the sun might be shining directly in your eyes in one lane, while the other lane might have shade. This could significantly affect your reaction time so it bears watching.

The Starter

Many people incorrectly assume that the starter's only duty is to flip the switch that activates the Christmas tree starting system. In fact, the starter might have the most important job at the race track. While the starter does in fact start each race, his or her job also includes checking the racing surface for fluids or debris. The job includes making sure that the previous competitors have left the track before starting the next race. The starter may also perform a quick visual check of each vehicle and its driver, checking for leaks and to make sure that the proper safety equipment, such as seat belts and helmets, are in place and correctly fastened.

Since the starter is usually the last person to have contact with the vehicle before it goes down the race track it's important that you always follow his or her instructions.

The starter also monitors the condition of the racing surface. Over the course of an event, it is common for the starting line to develop bald spots or areas where the rubber has lifted. Most tracks use a form of glue or traction compound on the starting line, which greatly increases traction. If

Here, a starting line official grooms the starting line by applying additional traction compound to a couple of bald spots that have developed. Bald spots occur when the layer of rubber that coats the starting line begins to peel. If there is a bald spot on the racing surface, drive around it and not through it. You don't want to spin and ruin your ET.

In addition to starting each race, the starter checks the racing surface for proper preparation. Here, the crew sprays the starting line with traction compound, a sticky glue-like substance that greatly enhances traction.

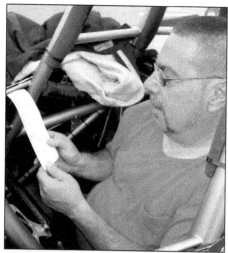

At the conclusion of each run you'll make a stop at the ET shack, where you will receive a time slip, which is essentially a report card of each run. Among other things, the time slip includes your reaction time, ET at various points on the race track, your top speed, and whether you won or lost. You should review your timing slips and pay close attention to your reaction times, so you can determine how close you are to a perfect light. In addition, keep all your timing slips available and organized so you can learn from your past performances and determine how you can improve.

bald spots are developing, the starter will often take a few moments to apply additional traction compound.

ET Shack Workers (Time Slip Booth)

At the conclusion of a run, the next track workers who you'll encounter are those in the ET shack, which is normally a small building located on the return road, near the finish line. The workers' primary responsibility is to give each competitor an ET slip, which lists all the important data from each run such as ET, speed, and reaction time.

ET-shack workers are usually in radio contact with the starter and the timing-tower personnel, and may be in a position to notify a racer of a potential problem, such as a leak or a missing or damaged part on their race car.

Once eliminations begin, one very happy customer (the winner) and one not-so-happy customer (the loser) greet the time-slip booth workers. Drag racing is an emotional sport and after a tough loss you might be tempted to take out your frustrations on the first person you see, but try to

remember that they're just doing their job and really don't have a stake in who wins or loses. In other words, don't shoot the messenger.

Tower Personnel

The timing tower is the center of activity for the event, and houses a race director, an announcer, and at least one or two other individuals who are responsible for operating the timing system and keeping accurate records. The tower personnel may not be as visible as the starter or staging-lane director, and you may never see them face to face, but they are equally critical to the success of a drag racing event.

The race director is usually in radio contact with other event workers and officials including the tech director, staging lane director, and time-slip booth worker. The race director should be well versed in rules and regulations because he or she generally has the final say in any dispute.

Safety Crew

Hopefully, you'll never have to meet these people, but in an

Inside the timing tower, a number of workers help keep the event running smoothly. At least one tower worker is needed to input data into the track's main computer, which ensures accurate timing and record keeping.

The timing tower also houses the P.A. announcer. Today, most tracks have a radio transmitter so important announcements can be broadcasted on an AM or FM frequency. It is important to get a competition schedule at the beginning of the day so you can determine when you will run. This way you will know when to prepare your car, how much time you will have to work on it between rounds, and when to get into the staging lanes.

emergency situation, it's nice to know they're there. In most cases, the safety crew at local events will consist of fire fighters and emergency medical personnel. Insurance regulations mandate that every track have an ambulance and qualified medical personnel on staff during every event to handle emergencies. If you're racing at a track that doesn't have a properly trained and equipped safety crew in place, I'd strongly suggest racing somewhere else.

Basic Vehicle Prep (Safety and Performance)

As noted earlier, most street cars can be raced at local drag racing events with virtually no modifications. This means they will require only basic preparation on your part.

While it is perfectly acceptable to roll off the highway and onto the drag strip with your daily driver, you should always perform a basic safety inspection. Your routine inspection should include a check of tire wear and pressure, fluid levels, and a quick scan under the hood to look for potential problems such as a frayed belt or loose battery hold-down.

If you're looking to improve the performance or consistency of your car, there are a few simple things you can do once you arrive at the track. One of the most popular changes is to remove the rear tires in favor of a set of racing slicks or a set of multi-use DOT-type (Department of Transportation) street/strip tires. If your car is prone to tire spin, a set of slicks might well be the easiest and most cost-effective way to dramatically lower your ET.

There is an entire chapter devoted to tires later in this book, but if you're planning to use slicks

for the first time, a couple of words of caution are in order. First and foremost, slicks are designed solely for use on the race track and should never be used on the street. The handling characteristics of racing slicks are completely different from the street tires. They don't perform well in cornering or excessive braking, and if you happened to run across wet pavement, they're just plain dangerous. Even when used on the drag strip, racing slicks have a different feel to the way they handle and require time and practice to get used to.

Second, if you have a weak spot in your driveline, the surest way to find it is to bolt on a set of sticky racing slicks. Since slicks rarely spin, they tend to put a tremendous strain on driveshafts, U-joints, axles, transmissions, wheel studs, and other components. Many times, a racer has been pushed off the starting line because the combination of hot racing slicks and sticky starting line was too much for his or her stock Mustang, Camaro, or Honda Civic to handle.

Some racers also like to disconnect and/or remove their mufflers and exhaust system for improved

No matter what tires you're using, remember to make sure all lug nuts are properly tightened, and check your tire pressure before each run. You need to pay close attention to air pressure. Tire pressure directly affects how a tire hooks up and performs. Many racers will adjust air pressure levels within 1/4th- or 1/10th-lb increments during the initial runs, searching for maximum traction.

If you're looking to improve your car's performance, a set of race tires is one of the most cost-effective ways to do it. In order to run fast and consistent, you need to "hook up." A word of caution, though: A set of sticky slicks or multi-purpose DOT tires will hook up and place more stress on driveline components. As a result, weak transmissions, axles, and other components may fail.

Before making your first run, make a final check of your car for any signs of trouble, such as a leaking hose or frayed belt. You want to ensure that the car is ready to perform at its best so you can put up a fast, consistent run.

Before heading to the track for your first race, you need to do your homework. If you're racing at an NHRA Member Track, read the current NHRA Rulebook, which is published annually. If you're not racing at an NHRA Member Track, find and read the applicable rules. A properly prepared car will be quick, reliable, and consistent, but you also need to be sure your car conforms to all the safety and technical regulations. It's a waste of time to show up to a race and have your car thrown out at tech inspection because you missed something in the Rulebook.

performance. You should check with the track management to make sure this is permissible. There was a time when drag racing was all about noise, but today, that's not the case. The reality is that many tracks now have noise restrictions and some have only specific days when unmuffled cars are permitted to run.

Buy the Rulebook

Each year the National Hot Rod Association (NHRA) produces a Rulebook, which lists a complete set of guidelines for every class from ET brackets to Top Fuel. The Rulebook is considered the written authority about what is required and what is allowed when building or modifying a vehicle for drag racing. It is sent to active NHRA members each year as one of the many benefits that are included in the price of NHRA membership. You can go to NHRA.com to become a member. The Rulebook is an excellent source of information when building a car and it's also a very valuable item to have at the race track. Though it is primarily used to establish technical and safety rules for each class and vehicle, the NHRA rulebook also features a section on race procedures, which makes it helpful in resolving disputes.

The bottom line: It is a must-have item for even a casual racer. If you are not already an NHRA member, the NHRA Rulebook can be ordered online at http://store.nhra.com, by writing to 2035 Financial Way, Glendora, California 91741, or phoning 626-914-4761. It usually costs about $10. Also, changes between printings of the Rulebook are posted in *National Dragster* and at NHRA.com.

First-Time Expectations

To be blunt, one thing you should not expect during your first trip to the drag races is a victory, but you most likely will have a blast cutting your ride loose on a race track. While there certainly is something to be said for beginner's luck, and there are documented cases of competitors winning the first time out, the reality is that you will likely be racing against competitors who have much more experience than you do. Until you have made a few runs and accumulated some knowledge, you'll be the underdog.

With this in mind, don't be discouraged if you're eliminated early. Your first trip to the races is basically a learning experience and should be treated as such. If you happen to lose early, you might want to hang out and watch for a while. You can learn a lot just by sitting in the grandstands. In future chapters, we'll cover some basic mistakes made by beginners and how to recognize and reduce them. Like any other competitive endeavor, drag racing requires a lot of practice to be successful. Watching from the stands is helpful and a great way to gather information, but nothing beats on-the-job training.

Above all else, your first experience at the drag strip should be fun and should leave you wanting more. If you analyze your runs and learn from your mistakes you should quickly see an improvement, and before long, you'll begin to see the win light on in your lane.

Your first trip to the drag races should be a fun and rewarding experience, but drag racing is a complex endeavor, so it's unrealistic to expect instant success. There are many aspects of the sport to learn, such as setting up your car, properly launching the car, and driving the top end of the track. It's wise to treat the first few trips to the race track as learning experiences, so don't get discouraged if you're beaten in one of the early rounds of your first race. After you have learned how to run competitively, you can focus on winning.

HOW TO DRIVE

By now you should have a basic understanding of how a drag strip operates, and what you'll need to do to prepare for your first time at the track. Now, it's time to take you on a step-by-step journey through a typical run down the quarter-mile. Obviously no two vehicles are alike, and this means you will need to adjust your driving technique to suit your abilities and your car. Nevertheless, this chapter will give you a basic understanding of the things you should and should not do on a drag strip.

Later in this book, I'll cover in great detail subjects such as reaction time, dial-ins, racing strategy, and many other helpful hints. But for now, I am going to stick with the basics. Here, the focus is going to be getting you from the starting line to the finish line as quickly and as safely as you can.

Proper Warm-Up

In order to get optimal performance and longevity from your vehicle, it is important to have the fluids at the best temperature for racing. Engine temperature (especially engine-coolant temp) greatly affects the consistency of your car's ET, so every effort should be made to

Many sports require 90 percent preparation and 10 percent execution. When it comes to drag racing, the preparation to execution ratio is often higher. However, to post the desired ET, a skilled driving performance needs to follow often countless hours in the garage.

Checking your vehicle's vital signs, including engine temperature and oil pressure, should be part of every driver's pre race routine. Engine temperature can greatly affect the consistency that is critical to bracket racing success. If oil pressure decreases, the driver can quickly recognize that there is a problem so that catastrophic engine failure can be avoided.

maintain the same temperature run after run. In fact, monitoring engine temp is so critical, I'd strongly recommend a quality aftermarket temperature gauge as one of your first investments.

As you gain experience you'll find that running the vehicle with the engine cool, but with the transmission and rear at full operating temperature, will yield the quickest ETs. But as a beginner, just keep things consistent.

The engine isn't the only component that should be brought up to operating temperature. The transmission and differential/transaxle should also be kept at a consistent temperature. If you're driving a street car, you've probably put enough heat

At the start of each day, many racers place their car carefully on jack stands and warm the engine, transmission, and rear end. Bringing these critical components up to operating temperature reduces wear and tear on the driveline. In addition, this helps the driver produce similar, consistent times. This is also a good time to check for fluid leaks or other signs of trouble.

into the engine and driveline while driving to the track, so you might just want to let the engine run for a few minutes to bring it up to the proper operating temperature. If you've hauled your car to the track, you'll probably want to put the car carefully on jack stands and let it run in gear for a few minutes to warm the transmission, converter, and rear end.

Once your vehicle is properly warmed and you've completed all of your other pre-race chores such as checking tire pressure, making sure the fuel level is correct, and gathering all of your safety equipment, it's time to make your way to the staging lanes. As always, you should pay close attention to the staging-lane director and the track announcer, so you'll know when you are supposed to run.

Occasionally, you'll spend time warming your car in the pit area, and then sit in the staging lanes for an extended period of time. In all but the most extreme cases, transmissions and rear ends will retain enough heat to perform consistently while the engine can be fired for a few minutes just to make sure it remains in the proper temperature range.

At times, you might also encounter the opposite problem, which is too much heat. If your engine is running hotter than normal, it might be best to push the car through the staging lanes with the engine off until it cools to the proper temperature. Or, let it sit with the hood open to allow the engine to cool down before or between runs. If the engine is on the verge of overheating, you probably don't want to make a run and risk dumping coolant on the race track or severely damaging your engine. Even though a drag strip is only a quarter-mile or an eighth-mile long, your engine temperature is almost always going to be higher at the finish line than at the starting line. So if you suspect a problem, it's best not to take the risk. An alternative might be to figure out why the engine is operating outside of its normal temperature range and then come back and try again later.

Burnout Techniques

There is one thing to get out of the way right here: Long, smoky burnouts might look cool and they

At the race track, a burnout isn't performed for show or fun. A burnout improves traction in your lane, cleans off the tire surface, and puts some heat into the skins. Performed properly, a burnout will not only help improve your car's performance, but it will also help to produce consistent ETs, a must for bracket racing.

might impress the fans, but they are rarely necessary to achieve maximum traction. In most cases, it's just a waste of good (and expensive) rubber. A better alternative, one that is most often recommended by tire companies, is to spin the tires just enough to get them to start giving off a light blue haze. High-HP race cars usually require a more intense burnout, but for a street car, a shorter burnout is usually more than enough.

There are several good reasons for doing a burnout before each run. First off, modern drag-racing slicks and specially designed DOT-legal street/race tires feature a very soft rubber compound, so they're likely to pick up small rocks and other debris as you make your way through the pit area and the staging lanes. A burnout will help remove any foreign matter from the tires, so they have a good clean contact with the racing surface. Each burnout will also remove a small amount of rubber from the tire, creating a fresh patch to adhere to the race track.

Second, a burnout also brings the tires up to their proper operating temperature. Engineers from the major tire manufacturers have spent many hours of research and development and untold numbers of dollars refining and improving the design of racing tires. They've designed tires to work within a certain temperature range, which is usually around 130 to 170 degrees Fahrenheit, and sometimes higher. A bit of experimentation is usually in order when determining how long your burnout should be. The best bet is to start with a short burnout and then make them progressively longer until you find the tire's "sweet spot," the temperature that will give you the best

performance. The idea is to clean the surface to bring up a fresh, new compound for you to launch on. This also means that the first "hit" on the tires will be the best one, so don't do any "dry hops" or practice launches.

If you're using street tires, it's okay to do a burnout but you should avoid driving through the water box. You should do your burnout on dry pavement because it's very easy for water to accumulate in the tread of a street tire, which might cause you to spin on the starting line. If you do a water burnout with street tires, water can also be sprayed into the fender wells and later drip down, which might also cause tire spin.

For drivers using street tires or street legal drag radials, a short burnout is usually all that is necessary to achieve maximum performance. Most tire manufacturers recommend spinning the tires just enough to emit a light blue haze. If you overdo the burnout, you do nothing more than shorten the life of your tires. Since tires are some of the most expensive items associated with drag racing, this isn't a smart thing to do.

If you're using slicks, remember to first wet the tires in the water box and then pull forward until the drive tires are just slightly out of the water box before beginning your burnout. One of the most common mistakes novice racers make is to perform a burnout with the rear tires squarely in the middle of water box. The problem is you'll have to drive through a puddle of water in order to get to the starting line. The end result is that the tires remain wet, which is often far worse than not doing a burnout at all. Usually, the starter or another starting-line official will be there to help guide you into the proper position and give you the signal when it's safe to begin the burnout procedure.

Once a driver is properly positioned in the waterbox, he or she will often give the tires a quick spin to make sure the whole tire is covered in water. Once the track ahead is clear of the waterbox, the driver is given the signal to begin the burnout. You don't want to burn out too early in case the car ahead of you leaks water and forces you to wait while the track crew cleans up. Techniques vary greatly depending on the vehicle, the tires, transmission type, and other factors. The weather can also influence your burnout technique, since a cold race track will require a longer burnout in order to get the tires hot. Most race cars (at least those with front brakes) are equipped with a line lock, which is a device that holds the front brakes while allowing the rear tires to spin freely. Setting the line lock for a burnout usually consists of giving the brake pedal a few pumps to build pressure, then pushing the button to activate the line lock. With a line lock, the car will not move forward

Here is an example of a properly executed burnout. The driver begins by rolling all the way through the waterbox in order to get the whole tire wet. A driver should slowly idle through the waterbox to coat the tires with water.

Before beginning the burnout, the driver stops on the far side of the waterbox where the pavement is dry and clean. Never start your burnout with your rear tires sitting in water. If you make this rookie mistake and do a burnout in water, you may track water up to the starting line and certainly you will lose some credibility. There's a lot to take in at your first race, so be observant and careful. Make sure to check that your rear tires are out of the water.

When given the proper signal by a starting line official, it's time to put some heat into the massive rear slicks. Start with a short burnout. Your goal is to get the tires to produce a light blue haze and raise the operating temperature, usually between 130 to 170 degrees Fahrenheit. If more time is required to properly warm your tires, progressively increase the burnout time until you find the tire's "sweet spot."

When performing a burnout, one tire will occasionally gain more traction than the other, causing the vehicle to drift sideways. Abort the burnout if necessary to prevent the car from getting out of shape.

The burnout procedure for a front wheel drive vehicle differs slightly from a rear wheel drive car. Using the factory emergency brake, the driver locks the rear tires, so the front (drive) tires can be heated while the car remains stationary.

out of the water box until the driver releases the button. This makes it possible to achieve consistent results from one burnout to the next.

One of the secrets to a successful burnout is to build wheel speed because it will produce more friction and increase heat in the tires quicker. That's why most racers do not do their burnouts in a gear that allows for good wheel speed, but, rather, one that doesn't cause the engine to bog excessively. If your car is equipped with a manual transmission, do the burnout in second or third gear to get the tires spinning faster. If you've got an automatic transmission, try to shift quickly from first to second gear in order to achieve the same result. I recommend angling your side mirror at the driver's side tire so you can glance down and monitor the level of smoke you are generating.

Once you've got the tires spinning and you feel you've gotten the tires up to the proper operating temperature, stay on the gas and drive the vehicle out of the burnout under power. This will help make sure the tires stay hot and dry. During your burnout, it's also important not to over-rev the engine, which can cause damage to pistons, valves, and valvesprings. Try to work the throttle so that you achieve a consistent RPM level throughout the burnout. And don't bounce the throttle because this wreaks havoc on connecting rods and valvesprings.

If you're racing a front-wheel-drive car, the technique for performing a burnout differs slightly from the rear-wheel-drive technique. The car should be equipped with the factory emergency brake, so you can use it as sort of a "poor man's line lock," locking the rear wheels to keep the car stationary in the burnout area. As is the case with a rear-wheel-drive car, you will also want to pull forward to the front edge of the water in order to keep from dragging water to the starting line.

Remember, unless you're racing in a professional class, such as Top Fuel or Funny Car, it is almost never acceptable to cross the starting line under power on a burnout. In most cases, you shouldn't cross the starting line at all. However, Super Comp-style dragsters and other cars that aren't equipped with front brakes often coast a few feet across the starting line at the end of a burnout.

One final thing to remember regarding burnouts is to avoid holding up your opponent. It's extremely frustrating to be sitting on the starting line with your engine getting hot and your tires cooling off while your opponent takes his or her sweet time in the burnout box. If you take too long, the starter will probably give you a signal to speed it up, and if the starter doesn't say something, your opponent almost certainly will.

Staging and Launching

Proper staging is critical to success in any form of drag racing and requires great concentration and a significant amount of practice. Learning

Most stock-type vehicles use a line lock to lock the front brakes so a stationary burnout can be performed. A line lock allows the driver to lock the front brakes (or rear brakes in the case of a front wheel drive vehicle) and permits the rear tires to spin freely, so performing the burnout is easier and often more controlled. Line locks prevent "creep," which is useful because most tracks do not permit burnouts over the starting line.

Since most dragsters aren't equipped with front brakes, they generally do a rolling burnout but must be careful not to cross the starting line under power. At most events, only the top professional classes are allowed to perform a burnout and cross the starting line.

To make sure that you're properly lined up on the starting line, especially if you're in a car with limited visibility, have a crewmember guide you into position.

The key to improving your ETs is the ability to get your vehicle moving off the starting line as quickly and efficiently as possible. Therefore, your car needs to be up to operating temperature, in a good state of tune, and with its tires properly warmed, but that's only part of the equation. If your car is ready to perform at its best, you need to be ready to perform at your best, effectively cutting a light close to 0.400 or 0.500 seconds and dialing in the throttle.

As you approach the starting line, slowly inch forward until you light the amber pre stage bulb at the top of the Christmas tree.

The rollout, which is the measurement of the position of the pre stage and stage beams, is a critical component of reaction times. At most major events, the rollout is regularly checked to ensure consistent starting line conditions for all competitors.

how to properly stage and launch your vehicle is the single most important factor in achieving success on the drag strip. You will want to stage in exactly the same position every time. When you roll in and begin the staging process, a difference of even a quarter of an inch can have a big impact on your reaction time and your ET at the finish line.

If you're a novice racer, making your first trip to the track, you probably aren't going to be too worried about reaction time or how consistent your vehicle is, so you can relax a little and just concentrate on learning the basics of staging.

When you've finished your burnout you'll roll slowly towards the starting line. As you approach the line, you want to focus your attention on the Christmas tree, particularly the top yellow pre-stage light. Roll forward slowly until you light the pre-stage light and then stop. Now, you're just about 6 to 8

Pre stage: At this point you are only a few inches from the starting line and should be fully prepared to make a run. You have pre staged, rolling forward just far enough for the wheels to block the first beam and illuminate the pre stage light on the Christmas tree.

Stage: Slowly roll forward a few more inches to light the second stage bulb. The wheel and tire have now blocked both beams. The car is now fully staged and is in position to launch. At this point, a driver needs to be prepared to race and should be focused on the Christmas tree lights. When both lanes are fully staged, that is a signal to the starter to throw the switch that activates the Christmas tree lights. At this point, you should be completely focused on the lights in your lane.

Deep stage: If a driver elects to deep stage, he or she will do so by letting the car roll forward a few extra inches, just far enough to turn off the pre stage light. At this point, the vehicle needs to move just a fraction of an inch in order for the clocks to start. While deep staging can improve reaction times, it can also lead to more frequent red lights.

inches from being fully staged. This is the time to take a quick glance at your engine-temperature and oil-pressure gauges, checking for any obvious signs of a problem. It also helps to take a deep breath and to collect your thoughts.

Once you're ready, you can begin to slowly creep forward until you light the second stage light. If you're driving an automatic, use your left foot on the brake and your right foot on the throttle. Release the brake just enough to allow the car to move about 1 inch, then press back on the brake. This will give you the control you need to carefully and consistently stage. With a stick, ease off the clutch to achieve the same thing. If you have a line lock, you can apply slight pressure and drag the car into the beams. At this point, you should be ready to race and be fully focused on the stage light because once you are fully staged, that's a signal to the starter that its time to activate the Christmas tree.

The ET clocks won't start until your front tires break out of the stage beam, so staging the car shallow in the lights allows the front tires the chance to move a few inches before the clocks start. This often amounts to a tenth or two in free ET, but it can hurt reaction time, which we'll discuss later. Staging deep in the beam can slow your ET because the vehicle won't get a running start at the timing system. Once you have staged, hold the car as steady as possible to maintain consistency.

On your first few runs, you shouldn't be too worried about your reaction time, but you should still make an effort to get off the starting line as quickly as possible. After you've fully staged, you should focus on the bottom amber light on the Christmas tree. When you see that light come on, it's time to go. A common mistake made by beginners is to leave when the green light comes on. In order to get a competitive reaction time, you'll need to time your start so that your car is in motion just as the green light is coming on. That's because it takes a bit of time for your brain to signal your foot and for the car to react. Essentially, you want the vehicle to break the stage beam just as the green light comes on, and the only way to do this is to anticipate the green by leaving when the last amber light comes on. The launch is essential for making a successful run. If a car improves its 60-foot time by 2/10 second, the car will improve its quarter-mile time by approximately 4/10 second, if the entire run is clean. The entire range of times can be found at www.dragtimes.com.

Automatic Transmission Cars

If your car is equipped with an automatic transmission, you need to brake-torque or preload the drivetrain to effectively launch the car off the starting line. Essentially, the driver revs up the engine so it is loaded against the torque converter. To brake-torque the car, the driver must hold down the brake with his or her left foot and press down the throttle pedal with his or her right foot until the car starts to creep or the tires start to spin. When this happens, back off the throttle pedal slightly

Launch: Blink, blink, blink. On a standard sportsman or full tree, the lights come down one at a time, and in half second intervals. As a general rule, step on the throttle as soon as you see the third amber light come on. Some forms of racing, such as professional classes or Super Comp, Super Gas, and Super Street, use a pro tree in which all three lights come on at once.

while keeping firm pressure on the brake pedal. When the last row of amber lights on the Christmas tree lights up, release the brake pedal and progressively depress the throttle pedal until it reaches the floor.

Torque-braking is particular helpful for turbocharged cars because raising engine RPM increases boost pressure before starting-line launch, and increases HP output when the car is launched. However, torque-braking adds stress to the transmission and driveline, and you need to take this into account. It's a good idea for beginners to smoothly apply this technique and increase the RPM once more experience has been gained. Remember, this is an acquired skill and it's unrealistic to think that you will perfectly launch your car the first time.

As you are learning to race an automatic transmission car, you might opt to leave the transmission in drive and let the car shift by itself. You'll likely run a little quicker if you shift the car manually, but if you're not experienced, you might find it difficult to be consistent from run to run.

Manual Transmission Cars

If your car carries a manual transmission, the starting line launch procedure is significantly different from the brake-torquing technique for automatics. Using a combination of throttle and clutch slipping, the driver's goal is to launch the car at the ideal RPM and avoid wheelspin. To effectively do this, press the clutch all the way to the floor with your left foot, and at same time, push down the throttle pedal with your right foot until RPM comes up to the ideal level for launch. Every engine produces maximum power at a different RPM. You need to find out what that RPM is, so you can most effectively launch the car (a chassis-dyno run, discussed later in this book, will tell you the RPM at which the car produces maximum power).

With the left foot, let out the clutch pedal until the clutch starts engaging. Push the clutch pedal slightly in and wait for the Christmas tree to count down. When the last set of amber lights on the Christmas tree lights up, progressively release the clutch and apply more pressure to the throttle pedal. A quick launch usually requires some slipping of the clutch and some wheelspin. If you experience excessive wheelspin, you need to back off the throttle, so you don't ruin your ET.

You have the responsibility of working the clutch pedal with your left foot while trying to hit your shift points cleanly. Identify the RPM where the engine produces maximum power. With many engines, this RPM level is near the redline. Shift the car in the powerband's sweet spot, so you post a fast and consistent run. As with automatic transmissions, this is an acquired skill and this will require a fair amount of experimentation before you find the ideal combination of clutch and throttle. However, every run provides a learning opportunity, so your starting technique should improve with more experience.

The Run

Once you leave the starting line, keep the car pointed straight and in the center of the lane. If you feel the car spinning the tires, or if the car is moving sideways, you may have to back off the throttle for an instant until you gain traction again. Most tires, and even good racing slicks, are prone to spinning at times, so a little movement is to be expected. However, if the tires are spinning, and the car is bordering on the edge of control, your best bet is to get off the throttle before you have a major problem. Ultimately, you'll probably need to make a few runs to acquire that "seat of the pants" feel for what the car is doing. You'll also want to listen for any unusual sounds coming from the engine or driveline that

The run is where the real fun begins. When you leave the starting line, focus your attention on driving the car by maintaining control and hitting the optimal shift points on time.

might indicate a problem. Again, if you suspect that something is wrong, or if the sudden acceleration has you confused or disoriented, just abort the run and coast across the finish line. Keep in mind, you don't have to impress anyone.

Remember your high school driver education classes in which you were taught to constantly scan ahead? The same principle applies to driving on a drag strip. You'll want to focus your attention down the track, so you'll have an awareness of the finish line. This concept also helps you to keep the car pointed in a straight line. This looking ahead becomes more and more important as you race in progressively faster cars. Racers who drive Top Fuel cars at over 300 mph aren't staring at the gauges or even looking at the front wheels when they leave the starting line. Rather, they focus their attention on the finish line because they need to concentrate on the track ahead of them. In drag racing, the speeds are extremely high and the driver needs to process the information and make decisions at the correct times. Think of it as aiming a rifle, and you'll begin to the grasp the concept.

This is the driver's eye view of the track. As you head toward the finish line, keep the car in the center of the lane since that's where the best traction is usually found. As long as your car is running well and you feel comfortable, hold the throttle to the floor and enjoy the ride.

Assuming that your car is performing well and you feel comfortable driving, keep the throttle held firmly to the floor as the finish line approaches. At most tracks, a set of cones, a stripe painted across the pavement, or some other type of marker clearly marks the finish line. At most tracks, the finish line is easy to find because that's where the scoreboards are located, but that isn't always the case. There have been many instances of drivers, even experienced drivers, shutting off too soon, or driving under power well past the finish line, because they wrongfully assumed that the scoreboards marked the finish line. The

bottom line is if you're not familiar with the layout of the track, you should do some advance scouting to make sure the finish line is exactly where you think it is.

Shutting Down

You should always remember that your run isn't over when you cross the finish line. You still must get your vehicle safely slowed and off the race track in a safe manner. By the time you approach the finish line, even in an eighth mile race, you're almost certainly going faster than the posted speed limit on your local freeway, and if you're driving a modified vehicle, you can easily be traveling at 100 mph or faster. At those speeds, things can happen in a hurry, so you should always be prepared. In fact, accidents can and do occur in the shutdown area, so you need to be just as careful here as on the rest of the dragstrip.

As soon as you cross the finish line, begin the process of slowing your vehicle. One thing you don't want to do is slam on the brakes. You want to avoid locking up the brakes and skidding the tires, which is unsafe and usually unnecessary. In an

As you approach the finish line, it's time to start thinking about bringing your car to a safe stop. If you are competing in eliminations, you'll also want to know where your opponent's car is in relation to your car. Most bracket races are won or lost at the finish line—this topic is covered in depth in later chapters.

At most tracks, the finish line is clearly marked, so you should know when to get off the throttle and begin applying the brakes. You need to firmly apply the brakes, but do not brake too aggressively and lock up the wheels. If you lock up the wheels, you could put the car into a slide and lose control. In addition, you could flat spot the tires, and this will cost you a new set of tires. Besides, it's another rookie mistake you want to avoid.

actual elimination round during a bracket race, drivers will occasionally lock up the brakes before the finish line in order to avoid a breakout. That practice, known as "excessive braking," is not only dangerous, it's also against the rules. If track officials see smoke coming off your tires near the finish line, it can be grounds for disqualification. In most cases, you'll get a warning first, but offenders—especially repeat offenders—can be subject to disciplinary action.

A better method of getting your car slowed is to gradually and smoothly take your foot off the throttle, and then slowly and steadily apply pressure to the brake pedal until you've slowed to a safe speed, so you can take the turnout. You'll need to pay attention to the layout of the track so that you'll know where the turnout that leads to the return road is located. Most tracks have more than one exit from the shutdown area, so don't feel compelled to take the first one. There's nothing wrong with driving all the way to the end of the shutdown area and taking the last turnoff if you happen to be going too fast to make one of the first

ones. Never—under any circumstances—turn around and drive back up the drag strip.

When shutting down, you'll also want to know where your opponent is at all times. As a general rule, if vehicles exit to the left of the track, then the driver in the left lane has the right of way and vice versa. If you can't see your opponent, don't automatically assume that he or she is behind you. Most race cars have limited visibility and some shutdown

areas have reduced visibility at night, so don't change lanes until you're sure it's safe to do so. Remember, never turn in front of another car.

If there is an accident or some other sort of emergency involving you or your opponent, get your vehicle stopped as quickly as possible so that the safety crew can have clear access to the scene. In the event of a crash, you might be tempted to jump in and help with the rescue, but that job is best left to those with the proper training and experience. The best thing you can do is stay out of the way. At the same time, if you experience a problem or if your vehicle is stuck on the race track, get yourself to safety and notify a track official as quickly as possible.

It is necessary for you to be familiar with the procedures I have outlined, which are necessary to make a proper run on a drag strip. After you've completed your run, you can head back up the return road, where you'll receive your time slip before heading back to the pits in order to prepare for the next run.

In the shutdown area, pay close attention to your opponent since you will probably both be using the same lane to exit the track. You should also remember that the scoreboards aren't always placed directly at the finish line. If you're unfamiliar with a track, check out the finish line before making your first run.

SAFETY GEAR, VEHICLE PREP AND SMART RACING

In order to prevent a frantic thrash at the race track, it's often best to perform most of the maintenance on your vehicle while it's at home or in a well-equipped garage. You should complete regular maintenance routines and tuning procedures before you bring the car to the race track.

A serious drag racer needs to perform essential maintenance and tuning, so he or she is able to pull off quick and consistent runs, and do those runs safely. Most of the work should be done at home, so you only have fine tuning procedures to do at the track.

As any successful racer could tell you, all the driving talent in the world is worthless if you don't have the proper equipment underneath you. This is why it is critical to establish a regular maintenance routine and stick with it before and during every trip to the race track. By now you should already know that consistency and repetition (the ability to do the same thing time after time) is critical to success as a driver. You should also take that approach when it comes to maintaining your vehicle; establish a regular maintenance schedule and stick to it. In the end, a good maintenance program is one of those things that helps to separate the good racers from the also-rans.

It isn't an exaggeration to suggest that most races are won or lost before the vehicle ever gets to the track. A well-prepared vehicle will ultimately perform better, be more consistent, and (most important) is safer than one that is neglected. Remember, a thoughtfully planned and well-executed maintenance routine will allow you do concentrate most of your efforts on other important things, such as becoming the best driver you can be and winning races.

As we've said before, it is the responsibility of the participant, not NHRA or any track, to ensure that all safety equipment is approved and correctly installed, worn, maintained and used.

Essential Safety Equipment

Determining what safety equipment is essential depends on a variety of factors, most notably the performance of your vehicle. If you're racing your daily driver, you'll probably need nothing more than long pants, seat belts, and possibly a helmet in order to race.

Once you begin going quicker, the need for additional safety equipment rises accordingly. This section provides some basic information regarding safety equipment, but it is by no means a comprehensive guide to race-car safety. In order to be absolutely certain of what is and isn't required, your first priority should be obtaining a current copy of the NHRA Rulebook (or the rules from the applicable sanctioning body, if you're not racing NHRA) and reading it thoroughly. Note that utilizing additional safety equipment or safety-enhancing equipment is permitted under NHRA rules. The levels of safety equipment stated in the Rulebook are minimum prescribed levels for a particular type of competition and do not prohibit you from using additional safety equipment. Participants are encouraged to investigate the usefulness of additional safety devices for your type of competition.

Also note that sometimes equipment certified by or meeting the specification of a third party stan-

dard-setting organization, such as SFI, Snell, or the DOT, is required. Note that under no circumstances may any certified product be modified, altered, or in any way vary from the "as manufactured" condition. Such modifications or alterations void the certification and the offending equipment will not be accepted by NHRA.

Helmet

Per the NHRA Rulebook, a helmet is required for drivers of all cars running 13.99 seconds or quicker. In addition, as of January 1, 2007, NHRA rules require that all helmets must meet Snell K98, 2000, 2005, or SFI 31.1A, 31.2A, 31.1/2005, 41.1A, 41.2A, or 41.1/2005 specs. You'll want to check the sticker that is located on the inside of the helmet to make sure it meets the above criteria before buying.

Picking the right helmet isn't just a matter of finding one that looks cool, or buying the one that has the cheapest price tag. The old saying, "If you have a $10 head, wear a $10 helmet," certainly applies in this instance. Once again, adequate research is in order.

A good helmet should fit snugly without being uncomfortable. A helmet should not move around on your head. To verify proper and safe fit, slip the helmet on and firmly fasten the chin strap. Put your hand on

Under current NHRA rules, any driver whose vehicle runs 13.99 seconds or quicker must wear a helmet. It's up to you to choose the best helmet for your particular application but this is one area in which you shouldn't cut corners. You need to buy an SFI-rated helmet designed for car racing because it's designed for multiple impacts associated with car-racing accidents. The helmet needs to be acceptable for the type of car. For instance, if you're racing an open-cockpit car, you won't be able to wear an open-face helmet.

A helmet needs to fit properly so it provides excellent comfort and maximum protection. Therefore, it should fit snugly but not tightly and the eyeport should provide a wide field of vision. Before purchasing a helmet, check the NHRA Rulebook to make sure that it meets the current requirements, which can change from time to time. In addition, helmets need to be treated with care to maintain their protective properties. If the helmet has been handled roughly, its protective capacity may be compromised and it may not provide maximum protection in an accident.

In recent years, many drivers have chosen to use a HANS (head and neck support) or similar device, rather than a neck collar. The HANS device is a restraint system that essentially anchors the helmet to the driver's shoulders. A tether from the HANS device connects to the helmet, limiting the movement of the helmet in an accident and reducing the chance of head and neck injuries. In some of the faster classes, a head-and-neck support device is a mandatory piece of equipment.

Top Fuel racers typically wear (from left) an SFI-approved or Snell-rated helmet with a fire resistant head sock, a HANS head and neck restraint device, a neck collar, and an SFI-approved multi-layer fire suit.

the back of the helmet and push the helmet forward. If the helmet rolls down your forehead and over your eyes, it's too large. If a helmet is too large, it won't provide proper protection, and a helmet that's too small will be uncomfortable and can cause headaches. However, if a helmet is a little tight when new, it's okay because the padding inside the helmet is designed to conform to the shape of the user; it will most likely fit perfectly after it's been worn a few times. An improperly worn helmet will not only fail to provide proper protection in the event of an accident, but there is also a good chance that it will impair your vision—a potentially dangerous situation.

If you're driving a full-bodied car, you probably have the option of choosing an open-face or a full-face helmet. While an open-face helmet offers a certain degree of protection and generally offers unobstructed vision, I'd personally opt for the full-face model. It will likely offer greater protection in the case of an accident and likely be superior should you ever encounter a fire. Moreover, you'll be ready if rules were to change so that a full face helmet were

required. There are numerous helmet manufacturers that offer a wide array of designs, which can fit just about any budget, so it's probably wise to do some comparison shopping before making your purchase. You can find out just about anything you'd ever want to know about helmets by contacting the Snell Memorial Foundation at www.smf.org.

If your car runs between 11.00 seconds and 11.49 seconds, it's time to invest in a roll bar. For ETs quicker than 11.00, or speeds over 135 mph, a full roll cage and a window net are necessary. Once you reach this point, you will probably also need to have a driveshaft loop, transmission shield, heavy-duty aftermarket axles, and a safety harness.

Firesuits, Gloves, Shoes and Head Restraints

After you begin running in the 9s, you'll be required to invest in additional equipment, including a fire jacket, pants, and gloves. You should consider a neck collar and driving shoes and other protective gear. If you're going to be driving a dragster or other open-cockpit car, a pair of fire-retardant pants is also a must. Even if you're not required to wear these devices, it's always wise to use additional safety equipment, especially if you are close to 10-second quarter-mile times.

Jackets, shoes, gloves, and even racing underwear are available made out of special fire-resistant material, which provides the best protection available in the event of a fire. When it comes to fire jackets, your ETs and the type of vehicle you're racing will help determine what is right for you. As a general rule, drivers whose vehicles are supercharged or turbocharged will be

Depending on the type of car you race and its performance, fire-retardant clothing, including jackets, pants, shoes, gloves, and even underwear, may be required. This clothing is made of a special material intended to provide protection in the event of a fire. If you're required to wear this gear, you should opt for the two- or three-layer variety, which affords far better protection than single-layer gear.

If you're planning on running quicker than 11.49 seconds in the quarter-mile, it is necessary to install a roll bar, and if you're planning on running in the 10-second zone, a full roll cage is recommended. For bracket racers, many racing-parts suppliers offer full roll cage kits that can be fitted into most cars. In most cases, installing a roll cage requires removal of the entire interior except for the dash.

required to use thicker jackets and pants than those who drive naturally aspirated vehicles.

A drag racer should look for an SFI-5-rated two-layer or three-layer firesuit for optimal protection. Single layer suits that are used for road racing in many cases do not provide adequate protection. Select safety equipment from reputable safety gear manufacturers. Arm restraints are required for open-bodied vehicles running 11.99 seconds or quicker. If you're going to be running in the 9s, or over 135 mph, you'll also need an SFI-accepted neck collar. A HANS head and neck restraint system is also acceptable in lieu of a neck collar. As a general rule, cutting corners and trying to save a few bucks is never a good idea when it comes to safety equipment.

Roll Bars or Roll Cages

A roll bar can offer a great measure of protection and can be vital to avoiding serious injuries in an accident. Several chassis manufacturers offer a bolt-in roll-bar kit that can be used without having to make major modifications to your vehicle or rendering the backseat useless. If you're going to build an all-out race car, a full roll cage offers the maximum amount of protection and will help stiffen the chassis, which is often necessary in high-HP applications. Whether you decide that a simple bolt-in roll bar or a full-tube chassis is the right way to go for your particular application, remember that any roll bar/cage should be built so that it does not hinder your ability to enter and exit the car quickly and efficiently.

Installing a roll cage or a roll bar not only affords the driver a much higher degree of protection, it also provides a strong support structure that stiffens the chassis for improved traction, handling, and overall performance. Roll bars loop around the

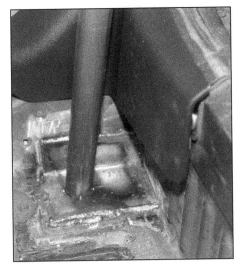

A properly installed roll cage has the added benefit of stiffening the chassis, which reduces chassis flexing when the car launches off the line. Gusset or mounting plates are welded to the floor to provide adequate reinforcement and then steel tubes are welded to the mounting plates. Typically, the stiffer chassis increases traction and lowers ETs.

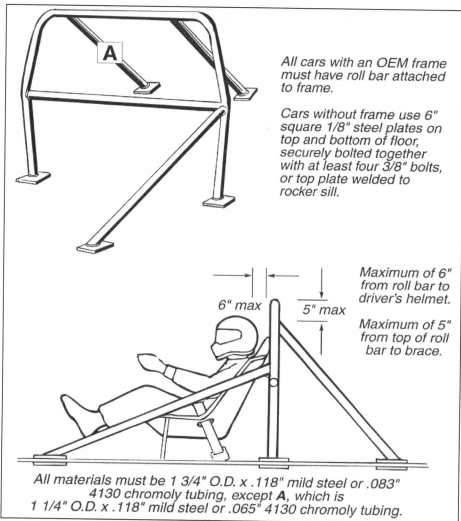

All cars with an OEM frame must have roll bar attached to frame.

Cars without frame use 6" square 1/8" steel plates on top and bottom of floor, securely bolted together with at least four 3/8" bolts, or top plate welded to rocker sill.

6" max

5" max

Maximum of 6" from roll bar to driver's helmet.

Maximum of 5" from top of roll bar to brace.

All materials must be 1 3/4" O.D. x .118" mild steel or .083" 4130 chromoly tubing, except **A**, which is 1 1/4" O.D. x .118" mild steel or .065" 4130 chromoly tubing.

The official NHRA Rulebook provides a helpful diagram and basic instructions that should be followed when installing a roll bar in your race car if you are racing NHRA. If you plan to install your own roll cage and are doing it for the first time, be careful and methodical. Remember to double-check all of your measurements before you start to cut and bend tubing. Each weld needs to be strong but not necessarily pretty.

roll bars will be welded to these plates, which will provide a solid foundation of support. According to current NHRA rules, the main roll bar can be no further than 6 inches behind the driver's head. From car to car, each roll-cage installation project is going to be somewhat different. You need to follow the installation directions and carefully plan and measure out tube length before cutting and fitting. Tack weld all the tubes in place before completely welding them to the chassis. With roll cages, solid welds are very crucial. Once the roll cage has been installed, paint the roll cage and reinstall the interior.

Safety Harness Installation

When installing a harness, make sure to follow the manufacturer's recommendations for proper installation

Many of the sport's quickest full-bodied cars, such as Pro Stock and Pro Mod cars, incorporate a Funny Car-style roll cage into the chassis for more protection. This particular cockpit includes additional safety features such as a five-point harness, window net, roll bar padding, and a custom fitted seat.

roof and in most cases conveniently install to the floor.

A full roll cage requires extensive work to properly install and often requires complete removal of the interior. Before you go out and buy a kit or tube stock, refer to the NHRA Rulebook (or other applicable rules if you are not racing NHRA), so you're sure that the roll cage or roll bar conforms to the circuit's rules. You don't want to install a roll cage and find

out later that it doesn't meet the required standards. Many race-parts suppliers offer roll-cage kits for a variety of popular muscle and sports cars. In many cases, it makes more sense to buy a roll-cage kit because it doesn't cost much more than fabricating one out of tube stock.

Full-frame cars provide great anchor points for the roll cage, while unibody cars often require metal brace plates for reinforcement. The

and usage. When it comes to selecting a safety harness, you should first reference the NHRA Rulebook if you are racing NHRA, or the other applicable rules if you are not, to make sure that the harness is suitable for the type of vehicle you're racing and its projected performance. A safety harness provides superior restraint, and therefore greater protection, than an OEM lap and shoulder belt.

Even if you're not running 11.49 seconds in the quarter-mile, installing a safety harness system is a good idea. You should install a five- or six-point system that includes a sub-belt. These sub- or crotch-belts prevent the driver from sliding down the seat in the event of a collision and allow the pelvis to absorb the energy of the impact, which often helps prevent injuries. The width of the belt or the use of a roll cage determines whether the shoulder belts are mounted to the floor or to the cross bar on the roll bar. The harness belts attach to I-bolts with washers or backing plates, which are mounted to different parts of the floorboards and chassis. Always use Grade-8 bolts for the attachment hardware. You need to achieve a proper fit and minimize belt stretching. Mount the belts so the straps do not rub on any components and be sure to keep movement at a minimum.

Safety belts generally are used for two years and then replaced. If the safety belts show any signs of fraying, damage, or unusual wear, or go through an accident, replace them immediately with new ones. Each safety-belt kit will provide specific illustrations and details for properly installing the harness to your particular car. Always follow manufacturer's instructions. Improperly mounted seats belts can lead to serious injury or worse. A properly worn safety harness should feature a lap belt that fits snugly over the hips; a shoulder harness that should be pulled tight to limit upper body movement; and a properly mounted sub-belt that prevents the driver from sliding down the seat.

Seat belts deteriorate over time and especially need to be protected from the sun. If your car sits in a shop, this isn't a problem. If your car sits outside and is exposed to the sun, the belts should be removed between races. As always, never take chances by using substandard safety equipment. No matter what you decide, remember that SFI-accepted seat belts or a full safety harness must either be replaced or re-certified every two years.

Brakes and Parachutes

Even though you only use them for a few seconds at a time; the brakes are one of the most critical components on your race car. You'll be traveling fast and needing to stop in a relatively short distance, so your brakes need to be reliable and they should be checked on a regular basis. Inspecting your brake drums or rotors and pads should be a vital part of your regular maintenance routine. If you're building a high-performance car, especially one that is an all-out race car, remember that you'll probably want to upgrade the braking system as well. A high-quality set of aftermarket disc brakes will not only increase your stopping power substantially, but they have the added advantage of being much lighter than stock brakes.

Per current NHRA rules, you won't be required to install a parachute until you're able to run over 150 mph in the quarter-mile.

A stock set of brakes is usually adequate for a dual-purpose street/strip car or a bracket car running slower than 11.00 seconds, but if you're planning on running much quicker, it is a good idea to upgrade to ceramic, metallic, or Kevlar-titanium aftermarket brakes. This is also a good way to save a few pounds when building a race car.

When building a race car, getting stopped safely is just as important as horsepower and acceleration, which is why you should pay particular attention to your vehicle's braking system. Oftentimes, an aftermarket master cylinder provides a significant upgrade over a stock unit, and it's easy to install.

Parachutes come in a variety of sizes and designs, so it is best to contact a reputable manufacturer for getting one that is properly suited to your particular application.

The use of a parachute also places tremendous strain on the vehicle so it is imperative that it be installed correctly. Bolting a parachute to a bumper or attaching it to the rear-end housing is a recipe for disaster. There have been numerous accidents caused by improperly mounted parachutes, including several in which the force of the opening parachute ripped the entire

A parachute must be securely mounted to the chassis. When deployed, a parachute will provide tremendous stopping power and place an enormous load on the car. If the parachute is mounted to the body or driveline, it can tear that piece off the car and create a potentially dangerous situation. This Pro Mod car also uses a net to prevent the parachute shroud lines from becoming tangled in the wheelie bars.

rear-end assembly out of the vehicle.

A proper parachute mount is one that is welded to the frame and is placed as low as possible. You must also make certain that the parachute shroud lines are the proper length, and that they do not interfere with the rear suspension or wheelie bars.

Like most other components, parachutes come in a wide variety of sizes and styles. When selecting a parachute, remember that the faster your vehicle is, the more stopping power you'll need to have. The weight of your vehicle should also be taken into consideration when choosing a parachute. Also, even if you don't need to use your parachute in order to get your car stopped, it's a good idea to use it from time to time because moisture can accumulate in the pack, which might keep it from properly deploying. You should also sprinkle talcum powder in your chute when you are packing it in order to keep the fabric from sticking together.

Once you've picked out the right

parachute for your vehicle and mounted it properly, take the time to learn how to use it correctly. First, you'll need to learn the correct way to pack your parachute. Different manufacturers recommend different procedures for packing parachutes, so be sure to follow their instructions to the letter.

Finally, you'll want to mount the parachute release lever or button somewhere where it will be easily accessible in the event of an emergency. At the same time, be sure to mount the release so that it won't accidentally be deployed during a run or when you're climbing into the car. There are enough other ways to lose a drag race without having to worry about your parachute accidentally deploying in the middle of a run.

Competition Driver's License

Under current NHRA rules, with a 9-second vehicle, you'll also need an NHRA Competition Driver's License. The procedure for acquiring a license

When packing a parachute, it's important to make sure that the shroud lines are not tangled. You should also inspect each panel for signs of wear or fatigue. If you detect any unusual or excessive wear, replace the chute. You simply can't risk a failure.

is fairly simple and straightforward. First, you'll need to contact the NHRA to get the correct forms. Next, you'll need to contact your doctor to schedule the required physical examination. At the track, you'll also be asked to take a cockpit orientation test where you'll be blindfolded and then asked to locate all of the switches and other controls of your car.

Finally, you'll need to make a total of six runs, including two starting-line launches, two moderate runs, and two full runs. You'll need to make these runs in the presence of a track official and two other licensed drivers who will then sign off on your license if you perform well.

The following is probably the most valuable advice that I or anyone else can give you with regard to safety, and you won't find it in any rule book. The two most important words to remember: common sense. If your car doesn't feel right going down the track, fix the problem before attempting to make another run. If something doesn't look right during your pre-race inspection, take the time to properly diagnose the problem and take the necessary steps to correct it. Or, pull out of the race. Remember, broken parts and other mechanical problems don't fix themselves. Take the time to do the job right before a small problem becomes a big problem. It's absolutely unacceptable to have the mindset, "I'll get around to fixing that sooner or later," or, "My car doesn't run that quick; I really don't need to worry about that." Remember, even a stock street car is most likely capable of running well over the interstate freeway speed limit on a drag strip, so it pays to devote substantial time and effort to maintain a race car.

Performing a Proper Safety Check

As noted in the beginning of this chapter, preparation for any event should begin at home. The most obvious things you can do at home include checking the hoses, belts, wiring, fluids (engine, transmission, and rear end), brakes, and header and intake bolts for leaks, cracks, or other signs of fatigue. Checking to

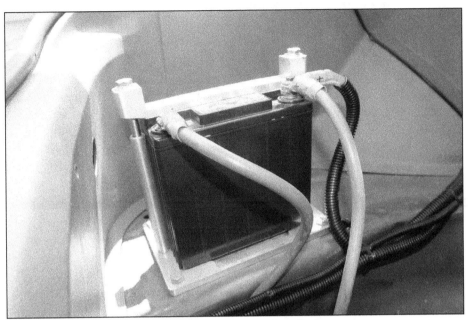

Often batteries are moved to the trunk for easy access or improved weight distribution. Whether it's under the hood or in the trunk, it needs to be securely fastened and properly ventilated.

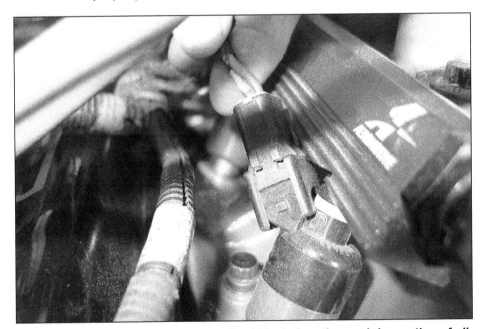

Your pre-race maintenance routine should include a thorough inspection of all wiring and electrical connections, hoses, and belts. You need to ensure that your car will perform, and perform safely.

make sure the intake manifold and carburetor are tightly fastened can also help prevent vacuum leaks that are sometimes difficult to detect, and will almost always affect your car's consistency. Whether it is mounted under the hood or in the trunk, make sure that your battery is properly secured.

A poor-running engine will lead to a loss of consistency and performance, so it's a good idea to make sure your engine is properly tuned. A set of fresh spark plugs, an oil change, an air filter, and correct timing are essential for performance and longevity so those items should also be added to your regular basic-maintenance list.

Loose hoses that could lead to fluid leaks should be repaired or replaced immediately. The same goes for worn or frayed wiring that could lead to a short or a fire. You should also periodically crawl under your car and check the suspension components and related hardware; these parts can loosen and/or wear out quickly even in moderately powered cars. You should check to make sure that all bolts are securely fastened, and that there are no cracks or other signs of fatigue. This procedure can be made much easier if you have access to a lift, but if you don't, a good set of quality jack stands and flat pavement should do the trick. Don't overlook the beating your car takes when being towed because this can often produce more suspension wear and tear than driving. Pay particular attention to the condition of your shock absorbers and struts because these items are subjected to significant stress while your vehicle is tied down tightly for towing, which prevents normal suspension travel.

Obviously tires wear at a much quicker rate on a race car, so a tire inspection is also a must and should be done after every race. I'll cover tires in depth in the next chapter but suffice it to say this is one critical component of your race car that should never be neglected. Any front or rear tire that shows excessive wear, such as cords that are visible or excess bald spots, should be replaced immediately. The same goes for any tire that is punctured by debris.

Finally, you should make it a habit to check your tire pressure on a regular basis. In most cases, you'll be constantly adjusting the pressure of your rear tires to provide maximum grip on the starting line, and many racers, especially those who race without the aid of delay boxes, use front tire pressure as a way of adjusting reaction times. Don't neglect your wheels either. Occasionally inspect them for dents or cracks and don't forget to check the tightness of your lug nuts.

Proper race car safety always includes attention to details. For instance, there should be nothing loose in the car that could cause injury in the event of an accident. While carrying a fire extinguisher in the car is a good idea, allowing it to flop around behind the driver's seat is not. It should be properly secured and easily accessible in the event of an emergency.

You'll be keeping a logbook to catalog your car's performance, and it's also a smart idea to make a checklist that includes all of your scheduled maintenance and stick to it. Once you establish a regular maintenance routine and begin keeping records, it should be easy to stick with it. After a while, it will become second nature.

Depending on your vehicle and how much time you have between runs, you may need to run cool water through the engine in order to help lower the temperature. Keeping the engine at its optimal operating temperature is very important for achieving consistent runs.

Between Rounds

Obviously, time is often limited at the track, so it's important to have a between-rounds maintenance routine that is both quick and effective. Top Fuel and Funny Car teams can completely tear down an engine and install a new crankshaft, new supercharger, eight rods and pistons, and have the car assembled and ready to race again in less than an hour. Thankfully, most of us won't have to thrash that hard between runs. More often than not, following a simple maintenance routine will have you ready to race again in no time.

Upon returning from a run, the first thing you'll do is monitor the engine temperature. Many racers use an electric fan to help cool their cars and will leave it running while the car is parked. If you're in the middle of eliminations and anticipate making another run in a short amount of time, you might also have to spray the radiator with water in order to help bring the engine temperature down to normal.

Tire pressure should also be checked and adjusted before each

Monitoring all of your engine's systems is vital to maintaining a consistent race car. In this example, the driver has a clear view of the tachometer, shift light, as well as oil pressure, water temperature, and fuel-pressure gauges.

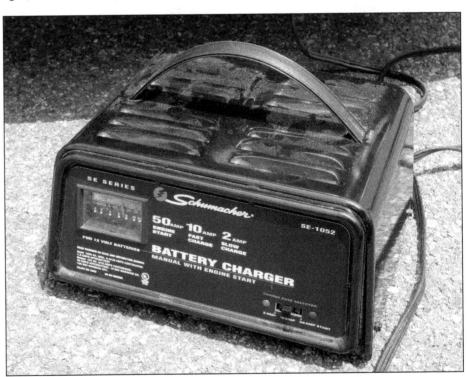

Monitor your car's battery charge after each race and charge it when necessary. If you are running a total-loss ignition, you need to pay particular attention to this. It hurts to lose a race because your car won't start. A basic portable battery charger can be essential at the races, especially if you're making multiple runs late in eliminations and your battery begins to lose its charge.

run. Remember, the pressure increases as a tire gets hotter, so if your car has been sitting out in the hot sun for a while, the tires will likely need a pressure adjustment.

If your car is equipped with an alternator, you probably won't need to worry about charging the battery, but for most real (non-street legal) race cars, having a generator and a battery charger at the ready is part of the regular routine.

Depending on your vehicle, you might also have to add fuel before each run. This probably isn't going to be necessary in a street car, but if you've got a small-capacity fuel cell or an aftermarket tank, it probably only holds a couple of gallons of fuel, so you'll want to monitor it closely. Keeping your fuel tank topped off will also help ensure that your car weighs the same from run to run, which will also help your consistency.

For those of you racing street cars, here is another tip to remember: If you make two or three time-trial runs and then go deep into eliminations, it's likely that your vehicle will use several gallons of fuel. Since a gallon of gas weighs roughly 6 lbs, your vehicle could lose 25 to 30 lbs during an event, which will make it run quicker ETs. If you began the race with a full tank, I wouldn't recommend filling it during eliminations, but you'll certainly want to consider this when selecting a dial-in.

Once you are certain that your vehicle is properly maintained and ready for the next run, it is a good idea to check the condition of the race track in order to better predict how your car will react. The track will change according to time of day and surface temperature. If you made your first run of the day in the overcast and cool morning and it is now bright and sunny, you are likely to find that the track, particularly the starting line, has changed dramatically. As a result, your car will almost certainly react differently. In this case, a tire-pressure adjustment might be in order, or perhaps you should add some additional weight (ballast) if you feel the car is likely to spin the tires. Again, the ballast, like anything else in the car, should not be loose, because that could cause a safety hazard.

Troubleshooting

Hopefully, your day at the races will be trouble free, but the unfortunate reality is that mechanical problems do occasionally crop up. In many instances, you'll be pressed for time so the ability to quickly diagnose and fix those problems is a must.

One of the most common problems that racers encounter is a defective starter. In most cases, a starter can be replaced very quickly, even between rounds, so it's a good idea to carry a spare with you at all times.

Electrical problems are also regular occurrences. Blown fuses, bad ground wires, and periodic engine misses are all common problems that you're likely to encounter at some point. Your toolbox should include a volt/ohm meter, a roll of electrical tape, some spare connectors and wire, and a good pair of electrical pliers. While you're at it, carry a spare set of spark plugs and plug wires as well since these items are easily replaced and can often provide a quick fix for a troublesome engine miss.

If your car is running rough, especially at idle, there is a good chance that the carburetor or fuel filter is clogged with debris. In this case, a can of carburetor cleaner might come in handy. If the problem is something else, such as a stuck

You should have a pre-race maintenance check list and closely follow it so you ensure that your car is safe and ready for competition. Before you make your run, don't forget to check the condition of the race track. Traction from lane to lane can vary throughout the day. The slower lane in the morning can be faster in the afternoon. This is especially important if you're racing there for the first time.

In most cases it's not necessary to bring every tool you own to the track, but you need to have some basic hand tools, such as ratchets and sockets, screwdrivers, hammers, pliers, and wrenches.

Whether you're fixing a problem or performing routine maintenance, you need to have the right tools for the job close at hand. Compile a list of the requisite tools and make sure you get them to the track.

If you encounter a mechanical problem at the races, take the time to diagnose the problem and fix it correctly. Don't cut corners or attempt a quick fix on a potentially serious problem. If you do, it could cause expensive damage and create a dangerous situation on the track. In addition, if your car is experiencing a problem, it's very difficult to post quick consistent runs, which are essential for competitively running in any bracket class.

float or clogged fuel injector, you'll likely have to remove the carburetor or injector. For this, you should have a spare set of gaskets handy, as well as a razor blade or gasket scraper so you can remove the old one.

Over the years, racers have done some miraculous things to fix a broken race car between rounds. It's common to see engines and/or transmissions swapped in less than an hour. I've also seen a flat rear slick remedied by installing a tube with the tire still on the rim, and the rim still on the car. The whole procedure took less than 10 minutes, and the racer went on to win the round. My point here is that just about anything is possible if you've got the proper tools, the right parts, and the know-how to get the job done. However, in the heat of battle, it is also easy to overlook a lot of important details. You may have been able to change that torque converter between runs, but did you take the time to make sure that all the bolts are tight? Are all the hoses securely fastened? Did you replace the fluids?

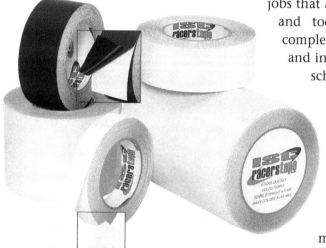

One low-cost item that can be priceless when making emergency repairs is a roll of good old racer's tape, also known as 200-mph tape. It's been used for thousands of repairs, so you should always have it on hand.

If you feel confident that you can pull off a quick repair job at the track and complete the job in a safe manner, then I say, "Go for it." However, realize that there are some jobs that are just too difficult and too involved to be completed properly, safely, and in time to make your schedule. Ask yourself, "Do I really want to pull that cylinder head if I'm pitted on dirt or gravel? Is it worth risking that expensive engine just to make one more run?" My point here is that sometimes it's better to throw in the towel and wait to race another day. A hasty repair might or might not correct the problem; or worse yet, it might result in a small problem becoming a big one.

Remember, common sense is key.

Necessary Tools

Hopefully, your trip to the race track will be trouble free, but as I've discussed in this chapter, that isn't always the case. You'll need to be prepared by bringing along a few basic tools and some other things that can help you get back on track if a mechanical problem should arise. Even if you don't experience a problem, you will have to perform some routine maintenance from time to time, and that will require tools as well.

As long as you aren't racing in Top Fuel, you won't need to completely rebuild your engine between rounds, so there is no need to bring a fully stocked rolling toolbox to the track. Many small problems can crop up, such as a loose bolt or wire, that can be easily fixed as long as you've got the right tools for the job.

A hand-tool assortment should include a complete standard or metric socket set, a ratchet, wrenches, a set of screwdrivers, pliers, vise grips, a tire iron, a hammer, and a torque wrench. A complete set of 3/8-inch and 1/2-inch-drive standard and deep-well sockets should be part of any drag racer's tool kit because you will need these for most maintenance and tuning procedures. Like your race car, your tools should also be inspected regularly to make sure they remain in working order. You need a high-quality dial air-pressure gauge with 1/10-lb increments that allows you to precisely adjust tires to various setups and track conditions. In addition, you need to bring an adequate-sized and charged air tank, so that you can fill the tires when necessary. If you're going to be moving tools back and forth from your garage into your trailer or race car

When working under a car, remember that a floor jack and a set of quality jack stands are mandatory. Don't crawl under a car that's only supported by a hydraulic floor jack. If the jack slips or fails, you could be crushed underneath the car.

Occasionally, you might need to perform some extensive repairs while at the race track, such as replacing an axle or a ring and pinion gear. High-stress parts in the driveline and other parts of the car can, and do, break when you least expect it. Be sure to bring tools to the track that allow you to change out the axle and make other parts that may break over the course of a weekend.

Being organized at the race track will go a long way towards helping you avoid a last-minute thrash if your vehicle should develop a problem. All of your tools, support equipment, and other necessary supplies should be neatly organized and readily available when needed.

each weekend, you'll definitely want a portable toolbox or tool chest.

Some other items that aren't so obvious would be a magnet for retrieving dropped bolts or washers; a magnifying glass to inspect spark plugs or other small parts; and, perhaps most important of all, a generous supply of duct tape, which is something no racer should ever leave home without. While we're on the subject of must-haves, a pair of safety glasses and some quality gloves are needed for protection. Before heading to the track, compile a list of all the tools required for setup, maintenance, and basic tuning and be sure to take all these tools to the track with you. It's always frustrating to be asking around the pits for a tool that you forgot, especially when you're in a time crunch to prepare a car for the next round.

If you're going to be changing tires, a good quality hydraulic floor jack is a must. If you're going to spend any time under the car, you'll also need to bring along a couple of quality jack stands, and some wheel chocks in case you are pitted on uneven pavement. While you're under the car, how about using a blanket, mat, or other pad? It will not only make things more comfortable, but will also make it easier to find any small parts that might get dropped.

Will you be racing at night? Then you'll probably want to bring along a flashlight or, better yet, a small generator and some portable work lights. Depending on the weather, a small portable heater or a cooling fan might also be in order.

At some time during the day, you're probably going to get your hands dirty, so a generous supply of hand cleaner, towels, and other cleaning supplies should also be added to your checklist.

A portable video camera is just one of the many tools that you should have with you whenever you go to the races. You can learn a lot about chassis tuning by watching how your car reacts on the starting line.

If you're going to be racing at night, it pays to invest in a good set of lights so you can properly prepare your vehicle between rounds. Every big-box retailer and most auto parts stores sell halogen work lamps for a very affordable price. You don't want to fumble around and waste valuable time because you are unable to clearly see what you are working on.

Safety on the race track shouldn't be your only concern. Getting to the track safely is also a priority. You need to make sure you're properly securing your car to the trailer. This car is properly tied down to the trailer in an X-pattern using a pair of heavy-duty straps, which prevent side-to-side movement.

It's important to keep your race trailer and pit area clean and organized. It will save you time when preparing your car for the next run and it will give you some peace of mind to know that your equipment is where you can find it.

ALL ABOUT TIRES

One of the features that makes drag racing distinguishable from other forms of motorsports is the huge rear tires or slicks that are used by most competitors. A drag-racing slick can measure more than 18 inches wide and more than 36 inches high. Slicks provide an enormous contact patch and sticky compound so the car is able to hook up and transmit its HP to the ground.

There is a very good reason why I have chosen to devote an entire chapter of this book to tires, and that is because there is no other single component that will have as great an effect on your vehicle's performance at the drag strip. The only parts of the vehicle that actually touch the race track are the tires, so no matter how much you spend on your car and no matter how much engineering has gone into it, you will not achieve the maximum performance until you select and use the right tires.

First, you have to decide which type of tires best suits your needs. If you're just bracket racing in mom and dad's grocery getter, you can probably get by without changing tires at all. However, for any kind of performance application, a fresh set of rubber is one of the easiest and

When building a race car, choosing the correct tire is one of the most critical decisions that you're likely to face. The correct tire can literally shave seconds off of your ETs.

For racers who drive their cars to the track, a drag radial (left) provides a big performance upgrade from a standard street tire. The drag radial features a soft compound so it provides ample traction, but it is also DOT-approved so it can be used on public roads.

Drag-racing slicks come in many different sizes and feature a variety of different compounds so finding a tire that is suitable for your particular application shouldn't be difficult. A slick increases traction and places more stress on the driveline. Therefore, it will expose weaknesses in transmissions and axles. Don't be surprised if you blow out an axle or another component if you run slicks.

most effective ways to lower your ET and improve consistency. This is especially true if your vehicle is going to be used solely on the drag strip. If that is the case, then a quality set of purpose-built drag racing slicks is always preferred.

If you are one of the many hobby racers who primarily drive their cars on the street but also make an occasional trip to the drag strip, a set of drag radials or DOT-approved "cheater slick" tires might be a viable option. As we've discussed before, when it comes to drag racing, the possibilities are endless so it is really up to you to determine which tire will work best for your particular application. The following information should help you make the right choice.

Racing Slicks

Purpose-built drag racing slicks have been available for more than 50 years and the engineering that goes into them, regarding both safety and performance, continues to improve year by year. In drag racing's early days, slicks featured a hard rubber compound and many cars, particularly high-HP ones, smoked the tires for nearly the full quarter-mile. Still, they were better than the alternative, which was usually street tires that offered less traction and less safety.

Tire Selection, Pressure and Maintenance

If you've decided that it's time to try a set of slicks, you'll now have to decide which ones are right for your particular application. Currently, there are a number of reputable manufacturers that produce tires specifically for drag racing and those

Some racers, such as NHRA Stock Eliminator drivers, use a radial slick during qualifying or class eliminations, and then switch to a bias-ply slick for eliminations. In most instances, the radial slick is quicker, but the bias tire is more consistent from run to run.

No matter what size tire you choose to run, it's crucial that it fits properly in the fender well. Remember that drag racing slicks expand at speed, so you'll need extra clearance to compensate.

manufacturers produce tires in many different sizes and compounds, so you have a wide selection to choose from.

One of the biggest mistakes that novice racers make is attempting to cure traction troubles simply by picking the biggest set of racing slicks that will fit under the rear wheel wells and bolting them on. Yes, replacing a standard passenger car tire with a sticky racing slick will almost certainly cure your tire-spin problem, but in order to achieve optimum performance, a little homework and some testing is probably in order.

It's important to make certain that the tire you've chosen will fit within the wheel well with sufficient clearance for tire growth. This is especially important if you are planning to use a bias-ply tire because they tend to expand at speed. Also keep in mind that a heavier car will require a stiffer sidewall, a bigger tire, and a tougher (harder) compound. Higher-HP cars should favor a larger tire.

First and foremost, you need to make sure that your vehicle has enough clearance to accommodate the tire you're using. Measure maximum wheel and tire clearance before you invest in a set of tires and head to the racetrack. It will save you a lot of trouble.

A typical drag-racing slick uses an extremely soft rubber compound for delivering maximum traction. Slicks are offered in both radial and bias-ply construction. Each one has its own unique characteristics. The bias-ply sidewall construction isn't as stiff as the radial, so the bias-ply tires will flex and wrinkle more than a radial. Therefore, the bias-ply tire's footprint changes or deforms under acceleration. The radial's stiffer sidewall construction features a more stable crown and a more consistent contact patch.

The best advice when selecting a tire is to talk with knowledgeable racers who are competing in your class or are racing a similar combination and attempt to gain some insights from them. Observe what the top racers in your class use for tires. As noted earlier, racing is a competitive sport, but most racers are more than willing to share information and are especially eager to help a novice racer.

While it's understandable that you don't want to have to buy three or four sets of tires, it also pays to be inquisitive when choosing a particular tire company. Even though most racing slicks are similar, performance can vary significantly from manufacturer to manufacturer and, in many cases, the only way to find the perfect tire for your particular application is by trial and error. Nearly all of the major manufactures of drag racing slicks, including Goodyear, Mickey Thompson, Hoosier, and Phoenix, have websites. They have tech experts who are available by phone and can answer just about any question you might have regarding your particular application.

Once you've selected a set of slicks, have each tire balanced (static balance is okay), and check the pressure. Measure and match the circumference (rollout) of each tire and make sure they are within 1/4 inch. While most manufacturers do a good job of making each tire the same size, there are often significant differences. A rollout mismatch can adversely affect handling, causing the car to drift to the side with the smaller tire.

When it comes to setting tire pressure, most manufacturers recommend setting the initial pressure so that the tread edges just barely touch the track surface. Then drop the pressure in 1/2- to 1-lb increments until you reach an optimum pressure for reaction time, starting line traction, top-end stability, and evenness of tread wear. As with any change, it's best to make one at a time and record everything in your logbook for future reference.

On a hot day, try raising your normal starting pressure by 1/4 lb and dropping it by 1/4 lb for a cold day. This is recommended because, even after a burnout, the internal tire pressure gains less on hot days and more on cold days.

On rare occasions, a racing slick will not properly adhere to the wheel, and the wheel will begin to move while the tire remains stationary. This problem, which is generally found only on high-HP applications, can be detected by placing a hash mark on the lower sidewall of the tire in line with the air valve. After you return from a run, check to see if the sidewall has moved in relation to the valve. If it has moved, you should follow the tire manufacturer's recommendation for installation of bead screws to hold the tire and wheel together. For vehicles that achieve speeds in excess of 200 mph,

A pencil air-pressure gauge may be adequate for a street car, but it's not as accurate as a high-quality dial air-pressure gauge, such as this one.

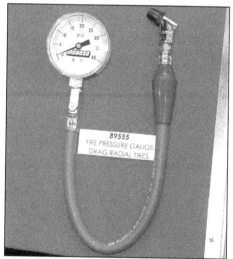

This gauge allows you to set air pressure within 1/10 of a lb. Air pressure greatly affects the performance of the tires and needs to be set to correct levels and closely monitored.

a bead-lock wheel is highly recommended.

How many runs you can expect to get out of a set of slicks depends on many factors. In general, tires used on lower HP cars will last longer. It is common for a weekend bracket racer to get more than 200 passes on a set of tires while a 6-second, 225-mph Pro Mod car may only get 8 to 12 passes (or less) before it's time for some new rubber.

To maximize tire life, don't do a burnout past the point where you see smoke; rotate your tires from side to side, at least three to four times over their expected life; and always make sure to run the correct air pressure.

Although the art of the burnout was covered in Chapter 3, it is such an important part of each run that much of it bears repeating. First off, keep in mind that the purpose of a

If you're using beadlock-type wheels, it's important to note that it will add a significant amount of rotating weight to your vehicle and will likely require a clutch and/or chassis adjustment.

burnout is to clean off the tires and to get the surface of the tire soft and sticky so that it can grab hold of the track surface. During the burnout process, heat is released so "getting heat into the tires" is not nearly as important as getting the tires to feel sticky to the touch after the burnout.

This heat is a by-product of the burnout process and is very quickly dissipated into the air. A burnout should be done consistently so that the surface of the tire will feel sticky. After the burnout the tire will quickly cool and be in the range of the track surface temperature. The infrared gun's best use is to determine the track temperature; a hotter track is generally poorer for traction.

As the track temperature increases, the tire tread will become softer so a much lighter burnout will

Many of drag racing's faster vehicles utilize a beadlock-type wheel, which uses a specially designed retaining ring that literally bolts the tire to the wheel. This keeps the tire and wheel properly sealed during hard acceleration.

Racing slicks need to be heated in order to work properly, which is why almost all racers perform a burnout prior to each run. A properly executed burnout heats the tires and removes any debris, providing the best possible traction. An overly aggressive burnout simply shortens the life of a rear set of tires. An inadequate burnout doesn't bring the tires up to optimal operating temperature, so the tires won't deliver maximum traction. It takes some time and experience to perform a good burnout, but novice drivers will get the feel for it.

be required to make the surface sticky. On cold days the tread will be harder, so it will take a longer burnout to melt the tire surface.

An excessive burnout will not get the tire any stickier and will only reduce tire life. In fact, it can actually destroy a new set of tires if the compound is soft and it starts to "ball up," i.e., the tire surface starts to break down into little round slivers of tread rubber.

Most manufacturers also discourage the practice of "dry hops" or "chirps," where the driver completes the normal burnout routine, and then performs one or more small quick dry burnouts before staging. Dry hops do nothing to help improve starting-line traction and place needless wear and tear on the driveline components. However, in some classes—Jr. Dragster, for example—dry burnouts are done as a way to control the engine RPM.

Selecting the right tire can help cure more problems than just excessive spin. For example, if you're trying to achieve quicker reaction times, you may want to try a bigger tire with a stiffer sidewall. Many years ago, racers in Super Comp and Super Gas realized that using tires with a very stiff sidewall helped them achieve the best reaction times. This is critical because obviously those racers compete using a 4/10 pro tree, and the ability to have nearly perfect reaction times is paramount to success.

If starting-line traction is the issue, you may need a softer compound or a tire with a wider footprint. The bottom line on racing tires is simple: When you get your first set of slicks, test and dial in the car on your new tires and remember to record as much data as you can. Keep stats for tire pressure, air and track temperature, length of burnout, and your vehicle's performance.

Depending on where you race and which class you choose to compete in, tire choice is occasionally not an option. In order to assure fair and balanced competition, some sanctioning bodies mandate the use of a spec tire, meaning that all competitors must run the same tire, including the brand, size, and compound. This can also be done in the interests of safety, as is the case with NHRA Top Fuel and Funny Car racers, who must run a spec'd Goodyear tire. In many cases, the purpose of a tire-size rule is to restrict the on-track performance of the car, specifically to hold down the speeds and help control costs.

Over the past decade, some of the most popular and most entertaining cars in all of drag racing have been the so-called 10.5 cars, which are restricted to a 10.5-inch-wide rear slick. Despite the size limitations, these cars are capable of performances in the 6-second range at speeds of over 200 mph. Interestingly enough, even though there may be a spec'd tire rule in place, some racers will try several different sets of the same tire in order to find the ones that perform best. For example, they may check the rollout of each tire looking for substantial differences. As a general rule, a shorter tire (one featuring less rollout) will be quicker than a tire with more rollout; although if track conditions are marginal, some teams may opt to go with the larger rollout. Remember, in a sport where wins and losses are often measured in thousandths of a second, every little bit counts.

Radial Versus Bias Ply

Slicks come in a wide variety of sizes and compounds also separated

A sticky drag-racing tire drastically reduces tire spin in most vehicles, but it can also transmit torque throughout the driveline, straining driveline components, so it's wise to make sure your transmission, torque converter, driveshaft, rear-end, and axles are strong enough to handle the traction from a slick tire. Otherwise, you may break the weakest link in the driveline during your run and will need a tow back to the pits.

If you're making the move from street tires to slicks, or to a multi-purpose drag radial, you should also consider upgrading suspension components including springs and shock absorbers. Since your tires are hooking up better, much more weight is being transferred to the rear suspension. A set of high-performance gas shocks will better regulate the transfer of weight and give the driver enhanced control.

into two categories, radial and bias ply. What is the difference between a radial and bias-ply slick? As far as handling characteristics, a radial slick is not as forgiving off the line as the same size bias tire, but it rolls more freely. For this reason, a radial is a better match for an automatic

transmission car, which doesn't hit the tires as hard off the line as does a manual-transmission car. Racers who compete in Super Stock and Stock eliminator will often favor a bias-ply tire because of its stability, but often these racers will switch to a radial during class eliminations, when they need to squeeze every last ounce of performance out of their vehicles. In the high-performance classes, such as Pro Modified or Pro Stock, a bias-ply tire is used exclusively.

The radial tire has essentially zero tire growth. You can actually see the differences in the shape of a radial compared to a bias tire during a burnout. In the bias tire, the tire profile will get rounder, and the tread width will become much narrower. The radial does not go through such a large shape change. Its profile stays essentially the same.

During the launch, both tires will "squat." In the bias tire the footprint will become wider and longer, essentially the reverse of what happens during a burnout. The radial tends to keep its original profile. The bias tire converts this enlarged footprint into more traction off the line. In addition, it will store up more energy in the sidewall by winding up and wrinkling when it squats during launch. These two factors account for the bias tire's better starting-line traction as compared to a radial.

In addition, the inherent sidewall construction of a radial is softer and more flexible. To maintain sufficient lateral stability, it requires about 50 percent more air pressure than its bias-ply counterpart. With a bias-ply tire, it's also important to note that when the tire grows, it will affect your car's performance. In essence, a tire that expands will have the same effect as lowering your gear ratio. Finally, the radial tire tends to wear faster, so the bias tire will usually last longer.

DOT-Approved Racing Tires

In the not-too-distant past, those of us who like to race our high-performance street cars had few options when it came to choosing a tire. Street tires, even a high-performance radial design, rarely provided enough

A high-performance street car or truck greatly benefits from the use of racing slicks. Unlike DOT tires used for racing, these tires are not built with compromises. Slicks provide a large contact patch, aggressive carcass construction, and a sticky compound specifically designed for racing. The F-150 Lightning gains so much traction from the slicks it picks up the front wheels.

Equipped with slicks, the Ford F-150 Lightning posts 10-second quarter-mile times, and uses a 9-inch-wide rear slick. Notice that there is practically zero tire spin and an impressive wheelstand.

Vehicles that compete in drag racing's faster classes, including Pro Stock, Pro Mod, and Comp Eliminator, rely almost exclusively on bias-ply rear slicks. The bias-ply tires are built with rubber-coated nylon or Kevlar plies.

traction for quick and consistent ETs. The alternative was to buy a set of slicks and a second set of rear wheels, and change tires at the track. For some racers, that is still the way to go, but in the past 10 years the line of distinction between a true radial racing slick and a DOT radial has been blurred because nearly all of the major tire manufacturers today offer some sort of DOT-approved drag radial.

While the tread compounds may be similar, the DOT tire will be slightly heavier than a true racing slick due to the addition of a thicker protective sidewall and extra sidewall stiffeners, which are necessary for lateral grip/stability during highway driving. Some extra rubber may also be added internally in order to help air retention.

Although these tires can be driven on the highway legally, keep in mind that the softer compound will run hotter and will not have the tread life of a normal tire. Also, after leaving the strip, remember to increase the inflation pressure to the recommended psi for highway driving; otherwise you can easily destroy a set of tires due to excessive heat.

DOT tires use a similar compound to that used in a true radial and do not need a long burnout. Once again, it's best to stop as soon as you see smoke and then promptly stage the car.

As far as pressures go, most manufacturers recommend something in the neighborhood of 11 to 14 psi for larger tire sizes, and 12 to 16 psi for smaller DOT radials. In most cases, the pressure range will be clearly listed on the tire's sidewall. Generally speaking, lighter cars can use pressures in the lower psi range, and heavier cars will need to use the higher pressures.

Obviously, DOT tires are more convenient than regular slicks and have been developed for class-specific applications. You can drive from your garage straight to the track and back home without the necessity of changing tires, but there is a compromise. While most DOT radials provide ample traction for all but the most radical street cars, they aren't as effective as a true drag-racing slick. Conversely, DOT radials don't provide the same handling, stopping ability, or longevity as a standard-performance passenger car tire. Although DOT radials are approved for street use, they are built with a minimal amount of grooving and do not channel water well, so they are not recommended for wet-weather driving.

Since DOT radials are made using a softer compound than a standard passenger-car tire, their lifespan isn't nearly as long. If you are going to race your street car and it is at all within your budget, I'd suggest having two sets of rear tires, one for everyday use and a quality set of drag radials that can be used on race days.

You should select a front tire that is rated for the speed you'll be driving. Choosing slightly different-sized front tires can significantly affect your reaction times.

While your rear tires do most of the work, it's important to pay attention to your front tires. It's a good idea to maintain high air pressure on the front tires, so rolling resistance will be minimized.

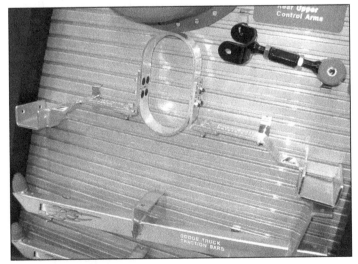

If you're going to be using high-performance tires, a driveshaft loop is highly recommended. A driveshaft loop is an important piece of safety equipment that helps to keep the driveshaft in place in the event of a U-joint failure. If the driveshaft fails and the car does not have a loop installed, the driveshaft will contact the track surface and could throw the car into a slide and/or damage the car.

To prevent sunlight from dramatically increasing tire pressure in a racing slick, it's highly recommended that you have a cover handy while your car is in the pit area or staging lanes.

IMPROVING PERFORMANCE

Hopefully, as you gain understanding of and experience with the basics of ET bracket racing, you've been able to put these lessons to good use at the race track. While everyone wants to win, true hot rodders have a burning desire to go faster. In this chapter, I am going to show how to do that. Because of the wide variety of vehicles and countless combinations that are available, this chapter won't be a step-by-step or "how-to" guide. Instead, it will feature some basic performance tips, which will help make your vehicle quicker and more consistent. Of

course, if you are racing at an NHRA Member Track, continue to consult the NHRA Rulebook during this process. If not, consult the rules of the sanctioning body that is associated with your track of choice.

Fortunately, improving performance is not that difficult and requires only a basic understanding of the mechanical aspects of your vehicle. Naturally, you'll want to start with a vehicle that is in good running order. For example, it should be equipped with new spark plugs, ignition wires, and cap and rotor (if the vehicle has a distributor). The engine

should also have good compression and top end, and not have too many miles on it. As a very basic rule, you probably shouldn't modify an engine with more than 80,000 miles on it. However, if the engine is in good running condition and you plan on making a few simple upgrades, you shouldn't have a problem.

Today, the aftermarket high-performance parts industry is stronger than ever, which means that finding

Drag racing holds a universal appeal for its many participants who enjoy the ongoing pursuit of lower ETs and faster top-end speeds.

Before you begin to modify any street car for racing, you should first make sure that it is mechanically sound. Most vehicles can benefit from simple items such as a fresh set of spark plugs and ignition wires.

Rather than modify an existing engine, some racers simply choose to buy one of the many readily available crate engines. Ford, GM, and Chrysler all offer a huge range of small- and big-block crate engines for a variety of applications, including drag racing. Often, a particular manufacturer's crate engines will directly bolt up to stock motor mounts on various cars and trucks in its product lines. Therefore, you do not have to fabricate non-stock engine mounts and fit the engine to the transmission.

Improving airflow into an engine is vital to improving performance so replacing a stock air-intake system with a free-flowing aftermarket unit is highly recommended. High-flow or cold-air intakes will increase HP across the powerband. Several manufacturers, including K&N, offer a wide range of aftermarket intakes for drag-racing applications. A stock system can be swapped out in favor of a high-flow in a matter of a few minutes.

power and performance has never been easier, no matter what vehicle you choose to race. When it comes to enhancing engine performance, you can take many routes. If your engine is old and tired, you may want to rebuild it or install a new engine. There are dozens of manufacturers offering "crate engines" and prices range from about $2,500 to well over $20,000 for state-of-the-art, big-block engines making over 1,000 hp.

Common Performance Upgrades

When your search for performance begins, the first place to look is the most obvious one—under the hood. Simple upgrades usually can be done in your family garage. These include improvements from installing a better-performing intake manifold and carburetor to adding a set of headers and a free-flowing exhaust system. Other common upgrades include a high-energy igni-

tion. If your plan is to spend most of the time at the track, you should also consider an electric water pump and fan, which will reduce parasitic drag on the engine. Here are some great ways to start.

Intake and Exhaust Modifications

Improving the airflow into and out of an engine is a great (and often inexpensive) way to start modifying your vehicle. Remove the restrictive factory air-cleaner assembly and

install a free-flowing setup from K&N or another reputable manufacturer. A free-flowing air filter and inlet tract can add 10 to 15 hp on many applications without affecting driveability.

Underdrive pulleys are another great way to add power. By reducing the RPM at which the water pump,

You should always a run a clean air filter because a dirty filter restricts air flow and reduces HP. A conscientious racer pays attention to these details and routinely performs maintenance. Independently, the benefits of these maintenance items may seem small, but collectively, it's possible to see a significant increase in performance. Also, the difference between winning and losing is often very small.

power steering, air conditioning, and air pump spin, there will be less parasitic drag on the engine, which frees up power to turn your tires. This is another modification that can be worth another 10 to 20 hp for very little cost.

In order to move more air through the engine, you can also look to the exhaust system for some performance. Installing headers (short- or long-style), a set of high-performance mufflers, and a compatible exhaust system will help to scavenge and utilize the exhaust gasses from the cylinders. When you improve scavenging, you reduce the pumping losses within the engine and also increase the amount of new mixture that enters the cylinders, thus resulting in a power gain.

Today's aftermarket mufflers are designed to not only decrease noise levels; in many cases they may actually help improve your car's performance. This is especially important because many race tracks now have noise restrictions and some limit the days when unmuffled cars can compete at all. Of course, when upgrading your exhaust system, you don't want to overlook the simple things like having proper ignition timing and the proper air/fuel ratio for your engine.

Carburetors and Fuel Injection

In order to complete the internal combustion process you will need fuel, air, and a spark. With that you also need to have a means of supplying the engine with fuel. While the fuel tank stores the fuel and the fuel pump supplies it to the engine, you still need a way of mixing the fuel with the incoming air in order to provide the most efficient means of combustion. Carburetors provide the ability to do this mixing and have

Some of the most common performance upgrades include the addition of an aftermarket carburetor and intake manifold. Selecting the right size carburetor for your car is crucial. If the carb is too small, the car will quickly accelerate but top-end speed will be significantly reduced because the engine is starved for fuel. If the carb is too big, it's being fed too much fuel; the engine will be sluggish and may bog off the line. In most cases, the engine will not cleanly accelerate until the engine reaches higher RPM. Therefore, the carb needs to be sized to match the air-flow requirements of the engine, or performance will suffer.

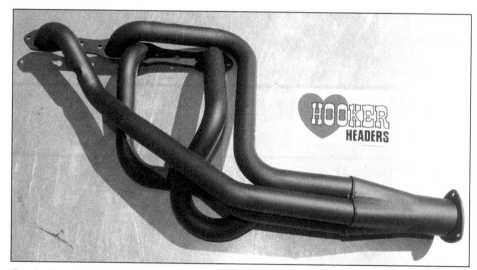

Replacing the stock exhaust manifolds with a quality set of headers can also produce significant power gains. A set of high-quality headers provides efficient scavenging, so unburned fuel returns to the combustion chamber. In addition, headers will provide a freer-flowing exhaust, so the engine will produce more HP.

Replacing a stock water pump with an electrically driven unit can help reduce parasitic drag on an engine and help to keep an engine cool when making multiple runs. Unlike a stock water pump that is belt-driven off the engine, an electric unit requires a fraction of the energy to run, and therefore is much more efficient. In turn, your car is capable of running faster ETs.

If you're planning on modifying your engine for drag racing, you should make certain that it's getting enough fuel. Replacing the stock fuel pump with a high-volume aftermarket unit is one of the first upgrades you should consider.

been around since the turn of the last century, but over the last 20 years or so almost every vehicle manufactured uses electronic fuel injection, simply known as EFI.

Most carburetors have a series of circuits to handle all the throttle positions, which includes idle, part throttle, and wide open throttle (WOT). When fuel reaches the carburetor it is stored in a fuel bowl. As the driver commands the engine to produce power in order to move the vehicle (by pressing the throttle

A properly tuned carburetor (or carburetors) should produce a consistent idle and a crisp throttle response. Inconsistent ETs can often be traced to carburetor problems. The engine must be able to idle, but for drag racing, you are tuning for best wide-open-throttle performance. Your target air/fuel ratio should be 12.5:1 to 13.0:1. If you're dialing in the carb at the track, you should make one change at a time and your car should be posting quicker times with each run.

pedal), the throttle blades (often known as butterflies) open and allow more air to enter the engine. As this occurs, there will be a pressure drop in the venturi, which draws fuel into the air stream. Fuel is pulled from the float bowls and is drawn through a series of jets and boosters, where it is atomized and pulled into the air stream. Atomization is critical because raw fuel in its liquid state will not burn very easily. Ideally, the mixture of air and fuel that enters your engine should be a fine mist, similar to what you'd get from a perfume dispenser.

Sizing your carburetor properly is important because it must be matched to the airflow needs of the engine, or performance will suffer. A properly tuned carburetor can do wonders to improve performance, but if your carburetor is severely out of adjustment, your vehicle might not idle or might not even start.

The displacement and operating RPM of the engine often determine the size of the carburetor. The goal is to create lots of air flow velocity to get the cylinder filled most effi-

ciently at all times. Various engines and different RPM levels affect the draw on the induction system, so there is no perfect carburetor for all engines. This draw begins in the cylinders as the pistons move down each bore on the intake stroke. As engine size (displacement) and/or RPM increases, the engine will require more air and a larger carburetor will be needed.

If the carburetor is too large, however, the draw or signal to the fuel system will be weak and throttle response will suffer. In contrast, if the carburetor is too small, the carburetor will become a choke point at high RPM. Sizing the carburetor on the small side may be advantageous in a street application because the result will be excellent throttle response from idle through the midrange. This will be due to a strong signal or draw that will cause excellent airflow velocity and efficient cylinder filling. In almost all cases, it's better to have a carburetor that is a bit too small than one that is too big.

Regardless of whether you have a carburetor or EFI, it is the job of

either system to properly mix the fuel with the air entering the engine into the proper air/fuel ratio. For naturally aspirated engines, this ratio should be from 12.5:1 (air/fuel) to 13.3:1 at wide open throttle.

This is easily monitored with an air/fuel ratio data-logging kit or by dyno tuning the engine. In many cases choosing carburetion will be the less expensive route, but it doesn't offer the tuneability of modern EFI. Since almost 100 percent of new cars have been fitted with EFI, your car may already have the system that should be cheaper to modify or tune. Even if you have an older car that came from the factory with a carburetor, you might benefit from a switch to EFI. There are quite a few manufacturers selling aftermarket EFI systems that give you total control of the fuel and timing curves as well as many other driveability factors.

With EFI, a throttle body meters the airflow into the engine, along with an intake manifold and individual fuel injectors that spray fuel directly into the air stream. An advantage of EFI is that since no fuel flows through the manifold, it can be designed with long runners yet still fit under the hood. Long runners are advantageous for low-to-midrange cylinder filling because they create a ram effect. As more RPM is required, the runners need to be shortened to achieve maximum power in that range. This is similar to the dual-plane carbureted intake manifold versus a single-plane version.

While there is no doubt that EFI is a more modern and more efficient way to mix fuel and air, many of the new carburetors, which are offered from manufacturers such as Holley

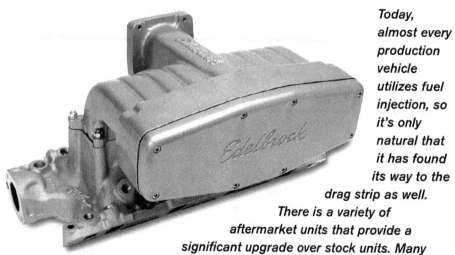

Today, almost every production vehicle utilizes fuel injection, so it's only natural that it has found its way to the drag strip as well. There is a variety of aftermarket units that provide a significant upgrade over stock units. Many manufacturers offer high-performance ignition chips that can be specifically tuned for a particular setup, track, and conditions. A laptop with ignition programming software allows you to burn a chip for your particular needs.

and Barry Grant, feature state-of-the-art technology. Additionally, there are many professional carburetor shops that specialize in custom tuning.

When it comes to EFI, popular manufacturers are Accel with its DFI, AEM, FAST, Big Stuff 3, MoTeC, Edelbrock, and a few others. Modern fuel injection allows a tuner to completely design a fuel map and timing map that suits the vehicle, whether it is being tuned for street driveability or uncompromised power. A street tune should be more conservative because the engine will generally see more heat and different fuels, and it must last longer. By backing off on the timing curve and running the fuel mix slightly rich, the engine will be protected against detonation.

Gearing

The next performance upgrade you might consider is to change your car's gearing. Since drag racing begins from a standing start, you will want gearing that will optimize acceleration. Overall gearing is affected by the gear ratios in the transmission, by the tire diameter, and by rear-end gearing.

Very often, optimal performance will require using a ratio that is numerically higher than stock, yet one that doesn't cause the engine to over-rev at the finish line. For instance, if your car is equipped with a 3.23 ring-and-pinion gear from the factory, a 4.10 ratio would greatly improve acceleration, resulting in much quicker ETs. It is common for a gear change to produce an

improvement of a half-second or more in quarter-mile ETs. Unlike the free-flowing intake and exhaust modifications discussed earlier, making a gear change will affect your

If you've chosen to modify your engine, it is vital that you also look to upgrade your transmission and torque converter. A rebuilt transmission and a new converter offer both improved performance and reliability. A purpose-built drag-racing transmission from Jerico, G-Force, or others provides stronger gear dogs, shift forks, and other internals. These transmissions are designed to handle the enormous loads of high-performance engines and the shock stresses of launching the car.

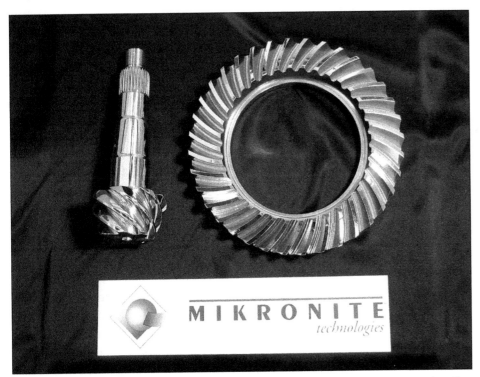

Changing your car's rear gear ratio can help to significantly improve acceleration and lower ETs, especially in the first half of the racetrack. For maximum effectiveness, it is important to select a ratio that allows the engine to stay within its powerband. Typically, a higher gear set is selected for maximizing acceleration. By identifying the RPM level at which peak HP is generated, and tire height, you can calculate the desired gear ratio for your car.

car's driveability. If your engine revs at 2,800 rpm at normal freeway speeds with a stock gear (say, a 3.23 ratio) then an upgrade to a 4.10 gear will likely cause your engine to rev higher, possibly 1,000 rpm or more at the same speed. The extra RPM isn't too much for most street cars to handle, though you'll almost certainly notice a drastic decrease in your gas mileage.

Moderate Performance Upgrades

If you've performed some of the modifications described above and are still seeking more power, the next level of performance will likely come from adding a high-performance camshaft and a set of professionally prepared cylinder heads. Obviously, these modifications mean that you'll be tearing into your engine and that your vehicle will likely be out of service for at least a few days, which is something to consider if your racer is

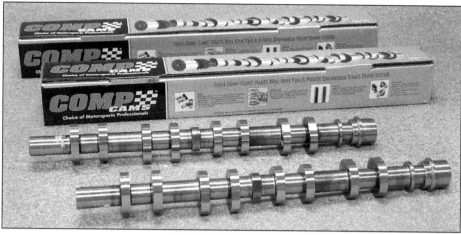

Camshafts are available in a wide variety of configurations to suit just about any application. You can select a hydraulic, solid lifter, or mechanical roller with varying degrees of lift. If you select a full-race cam, you will need a high-performance valvetrain to match the performance of the cam.

also your sole mode of transportation.

Once you've decided to take the plunge and install internal high-performance components, it's a good idea to check your valvespring pressure and make sure the valvesprings have the required pressure for an aftermarket cam. Weak valvesprings

will hurt power and can cause valve float in some cases. When valve float occurs, it's possible for the pistons to make contact with the valves, resulting in major engine damage.

No matter what modifications you're planning to do, I strongly recommend that you research your new combination of parts before making a purchase. Today, manufacturers and engine builders often have engine packages that they have designed and tested, so they know which parts work together to produce the best results. There are often several different levels of packages with carburetors and intakes, more complete packages that include the cam and valvesprings, and there are also kits that include new pistons, rods, gaskets, and bearings. Take the time to investigate which one works best for your particular combination and fits within your budget.

Also, remember that your combination isn't just your engine. It also includes gearing, tire choices, and the brakes. For instance, you wouldn't want to install a single-plane intake and a big 850-cfm carburetor

A high-lift camshaft and high-performance lifters will allow your engine to breath much better and produce more HP. Installing a high-lift camshaft requires removing the top end and selecting compatible rods and lifters.

on your street/strip car with a 3.55 rear gear ratio that will only turn a maximum of 6,000 rpm because you won't be able to fully realize the benefits of your intake and carburetor. In this case, a better choice might be a smaller 650-cfm carburetor and a dual-plane intake that will produce better torque in the low- to mid-gear range. If you swapped in 4.30 gears and have a manual transmission, the bigger carburetor and single-plane might be the best way to go.

Power Adders

If you're looking to make serious power, consider a power adder, such as nitrous oxide, a turbocharger, or a supercharger. These systems increase the level of oxygen in the cylinders to far beyond what can be drawn in

One of the most cost-effective ways to improve performance is with a nitrous oxide system. Simply, nitrous-oxide delivers 30 percent more oxygen into the engine, and therefore allows the intake to pack more fuel into the combustion chamber for generating a massive amount of HP. There is a wide range of nitrous-oxide systems available, including everything from an inexpensive plate to a full-fogger system.

simply by the atmospheric pressure exerted by Mother Nature.

Within our normal atmosphere, air pressure is usually measured at 14.7 psi. In your engine, when the pistons move rapidly down the bores on the intake stroke, a pressure drop occurs. When the intake valve opens, air rushes in to equalize the pressure. Therefore, filling the cylinders in a naturally aspirated engine is determined by the efficiency of the induction system and the barometric pressure.

With a supercharger or turbocharger, air is forced into the cylinders under pressure. We can then inject additional fuel to maintain the proper air/fuel ratio. Nitrous oxide is simply an oxygen-carrying agent, which is two parts nitrogen and one part oxygen. At about 565 degrees Fahrenheit (a temperature that occurs in the cylinder) the oxygen molecule separates from the nitrogen molecules and can then be used for combustion. This pure oxygen greatly enhances the mixture and additional fuel must be added to keep the air/fuel ratio in check.

By adding a turbocharger, supercharger, or nitrous oxide to your vehicle, it's easy to add anywhere

Years ago, turbochargers were a rarity in drag racing, but recent advances in technology have made turbos a viable option for many racers. Installing a turbo is a complex endeavor and complete turbo systems are rather expensive. Before undertaking a turbo installation, you need to carefully consider the cost-versus-performance benefit. However, a turbo will allow you to significantly increase performance without disassembling and modifying the top-end of the engine. A turbocharger also increases manifold pressure and places additional stress on an engine, which must be considered as well.

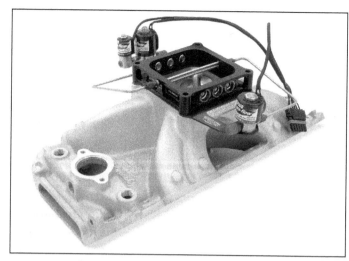

The most common nitrous-oxide systems feature a plate that mounts between the carburetor and intake manifold. The plate is fitted with nozzles that spray nitrous and fuel directly into the intake plenum. These systems are very affordable and are easy to install in the car. If you fit your car with nitrous oxide, precautions must be taken to avoid leaning out the engine and causing detonation, which could result in an engine seizure.

from 50 to over 500 hp to your engine! And in many cases, it can be done for a relatively small amount of money. Adding a supercharger kit to a new Mustang can increase the HP from 300 to over 500. However, you must first make sure that you have an engine that is capable of handling all that extra power.

Before adding any power-enhancing component, the engine must be in good working order. There is a plethora of power-adder kits designed to go on a stock engine and make lots of additional power. Generally speaking, if you plan to go beyond about a 125 to 150-hp gain, your engine will likely need to be fitted with forged pistons, better connecting rods, and a stronger crankshaft. It's possible to surpass the 500 to 600-hp mark with a stock long block, but a spot-on tune and careful operation of the engine is necessary to keep it alive.

A quick search of the Internet should reveal all types of power-adder kits, but common manufacturers include Edelbrock (nitrous), NOS (nitrous), Holley (nitrous), The

Nitrous Works, NX (nitrous), Magnusson (supercharger), ProCharger (supercharger), Paxton (supercharger), Vortech (supercharger), Whipple (supercharger), and B&M (supercharger).

Along with any power adder, you should consider an aftermarket ignition and, with all that power, you

may also want to consider a new clutch or aftermarket axles. Traction may also be an issue, so look into new tires for your ride.

Improving Performance Affordably

It's important to know that it doesn't take a fortune to improve your drag-strip performance. Sweating the details and learning what works and what doesn't can help you achieve your goals of quicker ET slips.

One of the simplest tricks that most racers are keen on is cooling the intake manifold prior to making a run. Since cold air equals HP, running with the engine as cold as possible will keep the intake charge cool, which also applies to the air entering the engine. By contrast, you also want the engine oil to be hot because this reduces internal friction, which in turn reduces parasitic losses.

As part of their pre-race routine, many drag racers, especially those in

Excessive heat is the enemy of any drag-racing engine. At the track, try to avoid idling and heat soaking the engine as much as possible. Cooling the intake manifold, either through the use of electric fans or ice packs, can be a very cheap and effective way to improve performance. You want to cool down the engine as much as possible between rounds.

performance-based classes such as Super Stock and Stock, will warm the engine before a run to bring the internal components and the engine oil up to proper operating temperature. In addition, they will cool the intake manifold using fans or by applying ice directly to the intake. Dropping the engine coolant temperature by as little as 10 degrees can often show a significant HP gain. With that, every 10 degrees will often show a linear gain in power. Many late-model cars have a big aluminum intake plenum and packing it with ice for 20 to 30 minutes before a run can drop the temperature by 30 to 50 degrees. This can be worth 10 to 15 hp in some applications!

Another cheap and effective trick is to use low-viscosity synthetic oil.

Once you begin to modify your engine, you'll most likely want to upgrade your cooling system as well. Any aftermarket aluminum radiator with dual-electric cooling fans should be adequate for all but the most radical engine combinations.

As a general rule, you'll want the engine as cool as possible and the engine oil as hot as possible before making a run. In NHRA-legal Super Stock and Stock cars, icing the intake alone can be worth as much as 0.05 second.

Not all of your tuning should be done at the racetrack, especially if you have access to a chassis dyno. A chassis dyno will provide a full range of information and help you identify how to improve performance before you get to the track. When building a race engine, a dynamometer can be extremely useful, not for just measuring HP, but also for finding potential problems.

After the run, a dyno chart will show how the engine makes power, and where in the RPM range it produces maximum HP and torque. This will help you determine how to drive and shift your car at the track.

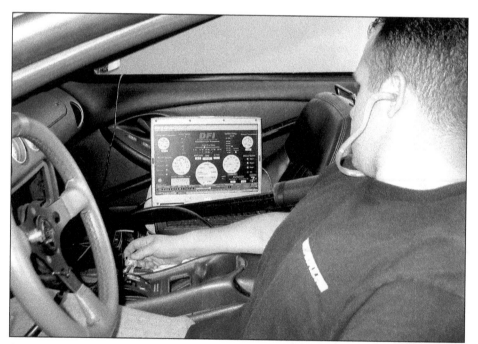

Just one session on a chassis dyno can yield enough data to produce significant performance gains. Some engines will produce a bell-shaped HP/ torque curve from a dyno run, while other engines show a steady climb of HP up the rev range with dips and peaks. With most street-oriented or production engines, HP will peak between 4,000 and 6,000 rpm and then HP will decrease at the top end of the rev range.

Trading that 20-50 weight for 5-20W can be worth substantial HP gains. Yet another trick is to run your engine a quart low; this gets the oil away from the crankshaft, and this trick can be worth as much as a tenth in the quarter. However, I wouldn't recommend this for street-driven vehicles.

A couple of zero-cost performance tips include pumping up the front tires to 40 psi (reduces rolling resistance), and removing the front anti-roll bar to save weight and enhance weight transfer. It is also recommended that you have a fully charged battery, and that your radiator is also full. On some engines, you can remove the stock accessory belt and replace it with one that only spins the alternator and the water pump. Eliminating the power steering, air conditioning, and the air pump will also free up more power.

Another way to generate more power is to tune your car on a modern chassis dyno. For about $150, you can strap your car down (which takes just a few minutes) and within a few pulls have great data on air/fuel ratio as well as HP and torque. Making changes to the tune by altering the ignition timing and/or fueling will show gains or losses in power at the rear wheels. It is common to unlock 10 to 20 hp on a modern car by altering the factory tune. In addition, dyno pulls will illustrate your engine's powerband and show you the RPM at which it is producing the most power. Therefore, you will know the optimal shift points for the car.

If you have a computer-controlled vehicle, you should consider a performance tune. Where performance chips were once the way to go, many manufacturers, such as Superchips Custom Tuning (SCT) and DiabloSport, now offer flash-tuners that plug into the OBD II service port and actually reprogram the car's computer with a specially designed performance tune-up. In addition, many performance shops can give you a custom tune that suits your equipment combination and driving style, and the climate that you drive in. And when combined with chassis-dyno tuning, you'll get some excellent results.

You can also do some major testing of parts on a chassis dyno, such as intake manifolds, headers, cams, and the like. The benefit is that you will be testing power at the wheels using your vehicle's components such as its ignition, fuel system, and driveline. Using this tool will show you if the engine is lean or rich, and where peak power occurs. This will tell you where to shift, or where not to shift.

To Use or Not Use Race Fuel

If you're racing a street car with a mild to moderate compression ratio, you most likely will not need to use high-octane racing fuel; in fact, it may even hamper your car's performance. Conversely, if your engine is modified and has a higher-than-stock compression ratio or highly advanced ignition timing, then you may find the need to increase the octane of the fuel you're using. In that case, there are plenty of race fuels that have increased octane.

Unlike the pump gas at your local station, specially blended race fuels often contain lead, which can damage oxygen sensors and cause your car's computer to run poorly. If your engine is stock, you can almost always get by on using 91–93-octane fuel or possibly adding a commercially available octane booster, which can help eliminate potentially damaging engine detonation.

Gasoline with increased octane burns slower than fuel with lower octane, and this inhibits detonation in engines with raised compression. As compression is raised over stock there will be more heat present in the combustion chamber. If it gets too hot, the fuel may pre-ignite before the spark plug fires the mixture, resulting in detonation (engine knock). Unfortunately, detonation leads to broken internal parts, so finding the best octane rating for your particular engine combination is critical. Most racing fuels start around 100 octane and fuels designed for use with nitrous oxide or other power adders can be rated at 118 octane or higher.

How to Improve Driving Performance

When it comes to getting the most performance from your ride at the drag strip, HP is just part of the equation. You'll also need traction, meaning a properly tuned suspension, and driver skills. In many cases, the latter is the most difficult to master. Nevertheless, there are some basic driving techniques that can help lower your ETs.

At the risk of being overly simple, you should first make sure that you have a comfortable seating position in your car. You will want to be seated in a way that not only affords good visibility, but one that will also allow you to have good leverage on the controls. Cruising down the freeway with your seat leaned backwards might look cool, but it's far from the best posture when operating a race car.

When you're racing, you should sit upright so that you can properly operate the shifter and the pedals. In some cases you may want to be closer than usual to the steering wheel, pedals, and shifter so that you can still rip the gears under acceleration. In addition, you need to be in a position where you can press the accelerator pedal flat to the floor. Again, this might seem like a no-brainer, but since you rarely press the throttle flat to the floor on the highway, you might not even realize that

If you've increased the compression ratio of your engine and/or performed extensive performance modifications, you most likely will need to use high-octane racing fuel. The machine shop or engine builder will likely recommend the ideal octane rating and fuel for the engine. A higher-octane fuel has a higher resistance to combustion and often remedies pinging. Every racer needs to eliminate detonation or pre-ignition, which can lead to catastrophic engine failure.

you can't reach the pedal until you get to the track.

Next, you will have to master the art the burnout. This was covered this in Chapter 3, but as a refresher, you want to spin the drive tires in order to remove any debris they may have picked up while driving in the pits. Also, you want to heat the tread slightly so the compound becomes soft and sticky.

After doing a modest burnout, put the transmission back into low gear before beginning your staging routine. Remember, dry hops aren't recommended because this will take the freshly prepared compound and use up the best traction on a practice launch, rather than on the real thing.

To achieve maximum performance you should stage the car as shallow as possible, meaning the front tires are just barely lighting the stage beam. This will give you the most rollout, essentially allowing the car to move forward about 6 inches before the timing system starts clocking your time. Shallow staging can equate to as much as 3/10 second free ET when compared to deep staging.

If you are using street tires, alter your launch RPM until you find the best 60-foot times. This may take some practice, so you should make about 5 to 10 runs before making major changes. This way you will know if you spun because the track was slippery or if it was your driving style or vehicle set-up. You can tune using tire pressure, shock adjustment (if you have adjustable dampers), and/or launch RPM. Remember, this is another area where proper record keeping can be very useful.

After the vehicle is under acceleration, you want to keep the car as straight as possible because weaving takes up time and scrubs speed. Sim-

ply put, the quickest route from point A to point B is always a straight line.

Whether you drive an automatic-equipped vehicle or one with a manual transmission, you want to shift a few hundred RPM above where the engine makes peak power. This will keep the engine within its optimal powerband for the duration of the run. Shifting at a low RPM can cause the engine to bog, while waiting too long to shift can cause the car to "nose over" or rev to a point where power falls off. It's also possible to over-rev an engine by waiting too long to shift.

While automatic transmissions shift on their own or with the click of a shifter, manual transmissions rely on driver skill. Those who can shift each gear quickly will achieve quicker ETs. Speed shifting or power shifting are two techniques commonly used by racers.

Speed shifting involves lifting off the throttle during each gear change, while power shifting constitutes up-shifting with the throttle pedal held wide open for the duration of the run. Power shifting is a learned technique. Moreover, if can't be done with every vehicle since some transmissions simply aren't designed to go into gear while the clutch is engaged.

For the best results, practice at a lower RPM, and then work your way up to the proper shift RPM. Basically, you will hold the throttle wide open while applying slight pressure on the shifter prior to the shift. Then, at the proper RPM, kick the clutch pedal and quickly move the shifter into the next gear. If done correctly, the engine RPM will only increase by 100 to 200 rpm. If the engine revs much higher than that, you need to practice.

As a general rule, there is a lot to be gained from practicing and refining your driving style. Racers often try different techniques for launch, as well as different shift points while searching for performance. Making many runs and keeping good records should also be a part of your performance plan.

Suspension Tuning Tips

The first thing a novice racer should recognize is that the chassis and the suspension are two different parts of the car. The chassis, or frame, is the foundation of the vehicle, and it will need to be both straight and strong. Some cars utilize a unibody frame, such as the Ford Mustang and the GM F-body vehicles. Many Dodge and Plymouth vehicles also have a unibody as well. What is a unibody? A unibody is a type of chassis that incorporates the frame of the vehicle into the body structure of the car. With this type of system, the suspension bolts directly to the unibody, while full-frame vehicles have an independent steel frame that attaches to the body. Many manufacturers favor unibody cars because they are often lighter and more cost-effective to build.

The suspension is comprised of control arms, springs, and shocks, sometimes called struts or dampers. There are also bushings and ball joints that allow the suspension to travel through their range of motion. In most cases, you'll find that the stock suspension links or arms are made from stamped steel, and the bushings are rubber. This is fine for a Sunday drive, but these parts can flex and distort under the extreme load of a drag-race launch.

To combat this, you can turn to the aftermarket for boxed or tubular control arms with polyurethane bushings. Some arms even have Heim joints or spherical rod ends and are adjustable in length. It is recommended that you reinforce the areas where the control arms attach to the rear and to the body or frame of the vehicle. This will ensure that the components work as designed for a long time to come.

To obtain good traction, you will need a loose front end with tall yet soft front springs that can store energy when compressed. Front shocks with a loose setting on the extension side allow these springs to work and for the nose to rise quickly and freely on launch to transfer the sprung weight to the rear. This weight transfer (called pitch rotation) helps to plant the rear tires and to keep them planted as the car accelerates.

In the rear of the car, you should consider using adjustable shocks attached to a braced or gusseted rear housing to prevent the axle tubes from moving, tearing, or twisting from the center of the housing. One problem many racers face is the rear

Any performance-related modifications you make to your vehicle should also be accompanied by a review and overhaul of your suspension. In many instances, stock suspension arms and components flex and twist under racing conditions, especially if the engine has been modified and is producing more HP. High-performance chrome-moly arms provide much greater strength, so the car tracks straighter during a run.

suspension reacting so quickly to the torque on launch that the tires will bite and then they will rebound and unload, causing wheelspin. To counter this, it's best to use adjustable shocks, dialed to a stiff setting. This will slow down the initial hit to the tires and allow them to remain planted.

In addition to understanding the basics, you should have quality front-end alignment and be sure that the rear housing is aligned properly

In order to maximize the effectiveness or any performance-related upgrades you make to your race car, you should also consider the appropriate suspension upgrades.

in the vehicle. Over time, your adjustments can become altered, and things can happen to cause links to bend or your chassis to flex. That's why it is important to install frame connectors if your car doesn't have them, and I also suggest installing a roll bar or roll cage, even if the rules don't require one for your vehicle. A

properly installed roll bar or cage connects to the chassis at several points. This significantly stiffens the chassis and allows the suspension parts to work as designed. If the chassis or frame is flexing when the power is applied, your suspension can bind or work inconsistently. This will be hard to see and can leave you

wondering why your car doesn't work well.

As torque increases from a modified engine or through gear multiplication, the forces on the rear housing and the suspension are also increased. Therefore, it is necessary to dial in the best suspension links, springs, and shocks for your vehicle. Almost all drag-racing cars should have the suspension links swapped out for aftermarket versions that are stiffer and have stiffer bushings to resist flexing. If the bushings are moving about, you will not see consistent movement from the suspension no matter how hard you try.

Weight Transfer

All the HP in the world isn't going to do you any good if you aren't able to apply it to the racetrack. This is why a complete evaluation of the car's chassis and suspension should accompany any engine performance upgrades.

Weight transfer is the key element that will help get your car up and moving while keeping the rear tires firmly stuck to the pavement.

On many full-bodied cars, wheelie bars act as an integral part of the chassis, meaning that they must be set at a specific height in order for the car to perform properly. Here, a crew makes a last minute wheelie bar adjustment just as their driver is preparing to stage.

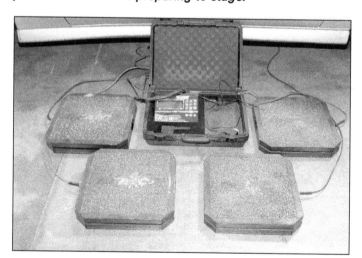

When setting up a chassis or troubleshooting handling problems, a set of four-corner scales can be useful to help set preload. A properly tuned chassis will have the weight evenly distributed to all four corners.

During a launch, the power from the engine will be transferred to the rear tires, but a lot takes place before the car actually begins to accelerate down the track. As the driveshaft begins to turn the pinion gear and the ring gear, the force will act as a lever on the rear housing. Next, the ring gear will begin to rotate, which moves the axles, wheels, and tires. Since every action has an opposite and equal reaction, as the rear tires rotate forward, the rear-end housing is being forced in the opposite direction.

Since the rear suspension is connected to the rear housing, the torque produced by the engine affects the suspension. For example, look at a car with a four-link rear suspension that's similar to a GM A-body or a late-model Mustang: As the rear housing rotates opposite of the tires, the upper bars in the suspension are pulled in one direction while the lower bars are pushed forward or slightly upward, depending on their angle. This allows the engine's torque to be transferred to the body or frame of the vehicle. In many cases, this torque transfer lifts the nose of the car, transferring weight to the rear as it drives forward. If enough weight is transferred, the car will go into a wheelstand, picking the front tires completely off the ground.

Moving a battery from the front of the car to the rear is a great way to improve weight transfer and traction. Remember, if the battery is in the driver's compartment, it must be properly vented to the outside of the vehicle. Whether you mount it in the driver's compartment or trunk, it must be properly tied down.

Here's a perfect example of how weight transfer affects a race car. The combination of sticky tires, a well-prepared racetrack, and a vehicle setup to transfer weight from the front to the back will often produce spectacular results. In this instance, this vehicle could probably benefit from the addition of a quality set of wheelie bars.

The key to getting a race car up and moving and keeping the rear tires stuck to the pavement is weight transfer. Your chassis and suspension need to effectively transfer weight under acceleration so the tires hook up and deliver maximum traction. Many times, you can find the correct balance in your vehicle by simply moving weight to the back of the car. An NHRA Super Stock car can have half its weight on the rear tires.

Carrying extra weight in the trunk is a great and cost effective way to improve traction. Since the rule book mandates that all ballast be properly secured, a specially designed ballast box is a useful addition. If you add ballast to the trunk, you will have more weight on the rear suspension and will need to adjust your suspension setup to accommodate the addition of this weight.

In the case of a vehicle that is equipped with a leaf-spring rear suspension, the rear part of the spring would pull the body or frame downward, while the front would see a lifting force, ultimately causing the same torque transfer effect as the four-link suspension.

When it comes to weight transfer, little things can make a big difference. For instance, moving a battery from the front of the car to the trunk is a simple operation that can take 30 to 40 lbs off the front of the car, where it hampers weight transfer, and apply it to the rear, where it can provide a great benefit. In a perfect world, you'd love to have more than 50 percent of the car's weight on the rear tires as some NHRA Super Stock and Stock racers do, but as a general rule, achieving that balance is very difficult and requires a lot of lightening of front-end components.

Building the Perfect Bracket Car

When it comes to building the ultimate car for bracket racing and streetability, there is no consensus of opinion for finding the perfect combination, but few would argue that two-time NHRA Pro Stock world champion Jeg Coughlin was not on the right track when he built his incredible 1967 Chevy II station wagon. At first glance, Coughlin's wagon might look like a vintage racer, but underneath its 40-plus-year-old steel body resides a state-of-the-art chassis and an amazing array of gadgets and creature comforts.

"In 2006, I decided to take a year off from Pro Stock racing and I wanted to build something that I could take to some of these big bracket races around the country, and I also wanted it to be street legal," said Coughlin. "I wanted something that was different, which is why I chose a Chevy II wagon. I've always liked the looks of these cars and I thought it would make a very cool race car."

Coughlin found the car he was looking for on a popular online auction site and bought it sight unseen. Over the next 12 months, Coughlin, along with fellow racer Kenny Underwood and the team from Jeg's High Performance, completely stripped the car and re-assembled it using a host of high-performance parts. After completing the body work, which included a new set of front fenders and a new hood, they installed a complete tube chassis and four-link rear suspension. The roll cage was specially designed so that it does not interfere with the driver or passenger's ability to get in and out of the car. The wheel

On the surface, Jeg Coughlin's Chevy Nova wagon may look like just another 40-year-old race car, but upon closer inspection, the car is a masterpiece of engineering and functionality. "It's also a heck of a lot of fun to drive," Coughlin adds.

tubs and other interior panels were then fabricated from steel. Coughlin decided to use steel rather than aluminum for both strength and improved sound deadening.

As one of the owners of Jeg's High Performance, Coughlin had literally millions of parts at his disposal, so he was able to select the best ones to suit his needs. When it came time to build the engine, Coughlin and Underwood decided to go with a 420-ci small-block Chevy, featuring a Dart block, Brodix cylinder heads, an Edelbrock intake, and a Holley carburetor that was modified for alcohol. Coughlin figures the car makes roughly 700 hp, not counting the additional 250-hp nitrous oxide system.

Since the car was built as a bracket racer/street car, Coughlin took steps to improve consistency, rather than focus on all-out performance. For example, the car is fitted with oversized Goodyear 33.5 x 17-inch rear slicks because, as Coughlin noted, "I wanted to make sure that I could race on any track without spinning the tires."

Built as a functional street-legal car, it carries all of the necessary components—a complete exhaust system, working headlights and taillights, a horn, and even a high-tech stereo system, complete with an MP3 player. The interior is also fitted with a set of comfortable seats, a custom-designed dashboard, and all of the necessary safety equipment for both driver and passenger.

"We installed a set of halogen headlights, and they've got high and low beams, just like any other street car," said Coughlin. "We also took the stock Chevy II taillights and put LED bulbs in them just to make them brighter. The button in the middle of the steering wheel activates the horn, except at wide open throttle, it then becomes the button that activates the nitrous oxide system."

A pair of delay boxes is another unique feature—one mounted is in the dash and another is in the glove compartment. There are also two separate transbrake buttons.

"We hooked the two delay boxes together with an interface unit so that both the driver and passenger could hit the tree, and the car would automatically take whichever reaction time is quicker. Obviously, the car is too fast to have a passenger, but I thought it might be a cool thing to have if I'm making an exhibition run with someone else in the passenger seat."

Building the Perfect Bracket Car CONTINUED

The spacious compartment in the back of the car is loaded with innovations including a 1000 kW generator, a battery charger, and a heating and air conditioning unit that uses a specially constructed duct system to funnel warm or cool air to the driver and passenger. The generator allows all of the extra components to operate without robbing power from the engine.

"We tried to make the car as simple and as efficient as possible," said Coughlin. "It was designed so that it could be street driven for an hour and then taken right to the drag strip with a minimal amount of preparation and maintenance."

Coughlin was tempted to complete the project with a flashy paint scheme, but ultimately choose to go with a flat black scheme. The flat black looks contemporary, and also has the added advantage of making it difficult for faster opponents to judge at the finish line, especially at night.

"When I'm bracket racing, I'm almost always the slower car so I need every advantage I can get," said Coughlin. "Fortunately, this car has a lot of window glass, so it's easy to look over your shoulder to see where your opponent is."

Running primarily on eighth-mile tracks, Coughlin is consistently in the 6.6-second range and has made the late rounds of several big bracket races. In August 2006, he demonstrated the car's driveability by participating in the annual Woodward Dream Cruise in Detroit, Michigan. Coughlin drove in bumper-to-bumper traffic for more than two hours with no signs of overheating or other problems.

For most of us, building a car as sophisticated and as innovative as Coughlin's Chevy II might be out of reach, both financially and mechanically. However, many of the car's features could easily be incorporated in any street/strip vehicle.

On the surface, Jeg Coughlin's Chevy Nova wagon may look like just another 40-year-old race car, but upon closer inspection, the car is a masterpiece of engineering and functionality. "It's also a heck of a lot of fun to drive," Coughlin adds.

The interior features comfortable seats, as well as a dash-mounted delay box and air shifter. There is also a complete stereo system with MP3 player. A full roll cage and twin safety harnesses help keep both driver and passenger safe.

The power for consistent low 10-second quarter-mile runs comes from a 421-ci small-block Chevy, which is fitted with Brodix cylinder heads, a Dart block, and a methanol-burning Holley Dominator carburetor. And if the 700 hp isn't enough, there is an additional 250 hp on tap with a complete nitrous oxide system.

Although Coughlin's Chevy wagon is fully street legal, the car does its best work at the dragstrip, turning in low 10-second elapsed times with very little maintenance between rounds. Built as a functional street-legal car, it carries all of the necessary components—a complete exhaust system,

The power for consistent low 10-second quarter-mile runs comes from a 421-ci small-block Chevy, which is fitted with Brodix cylinder heads, a Dart block, and a methanol-burning Holley Dominator carburetor. And if the 700 hp isn't enough, there is an additional 250 hp on tap with a complete nitrous oxide system.

The interior features comfortable seats, as well as a dash-mounted delay box and air shifter. There is also a complete stereo system with MP3 player. A full roll cage and twin safety harnesses help keep both driver and passenger safe.

working headlights and taillights, a horn, and even a high-tech stereo system, complete with an MP3 player. The interior is also fitted with a set of comfortable seats, a custom-designed dashboard, and all of the necessary safety equipment for both driver and passenger.

"We installed a set of halogen headlights, and they've got high and low beams, just like any other street car," said Coughlin. "We also took the stock Chevy II taillights and put LED bulbs in them just to make them brighter. The button in the middle of the steering wheel activates the horn, except at wide open throttle, it then becomes the button that activates the nitrous oxide system."

A pair of delay boxes is another unique feature—one mounted is in the dash and another is in the glove compartment. There are also two separate transbrake buttons.

"We hooked the two delay boxes together with an interface unit so that both the driver and passenger could hit the tree, and the car would automatically take whichever reaction time is quicker. Obviously, the car is too fast to have a passenger, but I thought it might be a cool thing to have if I'm making an exhibition run with someone else in the passenger seat."

The spacious compartment in the back of the car is loaded with innovations including a 1000 kW generator,

a battery charger, and a heating and air conditioning unit that uses a specially constructed duct system to funnel warm or cool air to the driver and passenger. The generator allows all of the extra components to operate without robbing power from the engine.

"We tried to make the car as simple and as efficient as possible," said Coughlin. "It was designed so that it could be street driven for an hour and then taken right to the drag strip with a minimal amount of preparation and maintenance."

Coughlin was tempted to complete the project with a flashy paint scheme, but ultimately choose to go with a flat black scheme. The flat black looks contemporary, and also has the added advantage of making it difficult for faster opponents to judge at the finish line, especially at night.

"When I'm bracket racing, I'm almost always the slower car so I need every advantage I can get," said Coughlin. "Fortunately, this car has a lot of window glass, so it's easy to look over your shoulder to see where your opponent is."

Running primarily on eighth-mile tracks, Coughlin is consistently in the 6.6-second range and has made the late rounds of several big bracket races. In August 2006, he demonstrated the car's driveability by participating in the annual Woodward Dream Cruise in Detroit, Michigan. Coughlin drove in bumper-to-bumper traffic for more than two hours with no signs of overheating or other problems.

For most of us, building a car as sophisticated and as innovative as Coughlin's Chevy II might be out of reach, both financially and mechanically. However, many of the car's features could easily be incorporated in any street/strip vehicle.

Although Coughlin's Chevy wagon is fully street legal, the car does its best work at the dragstrip, turning in low 10-second elapsed times with very little maintenance between rounds.

DRIVING AND TUNING AIDS

Would you like to become a better driver? Would you like to have a more consistent race car? Maybe you'd even like to find a way to make your car leave the starting line more efficiently, or you're having trouble selecting a dial-in and would like to be able to more accurately calculate the effect that air and track conditions have on your race car.

Equipped with all of the latest technology including a delay box, throttle stop, and air shifter, the cockpit of a modern-day Super Comp car might look very confusing, but an experienced driver has learned to skillfully use these driver aids to post quick, consistent runs.

For most of us, the answer to the above questions is obvious. After all, who wouldn't want to become a more successful racer? For those racers who are looking for an edge, or simply help in curtailing a recurring problem, such as frequent red lights, there are a large number of devices available that when used properly can help increase your chances of reaching the winner's circle. Some of the products currently available to racers include aftermarket tachometers, delay boxes, throttle stops, two-step ignition systems (rev limiters), air shifters, throttle stops, and weather stations.

Take a close look at the driver's compartment of almost any Super Comp or Super Gas car and you're likely to find a confusing array of wires, switches, levers, and digital readouts. With so much equipment crammed into such a small space, the cockpit tends to look more like a fighter jet than a race car.

The many gadgets that are currently available might cause you to wonder if some race cars aren't capable of driving themselves. As we're going to find out in this chapter, driving and tuning aids are no different from any other tool; they are only as effective as the person who is operating them. In other words, despite all the high-tech gadgets that are available from your favorite high-performance parts retailer, one that you aren't likely to find on any shelf or in any catalog is a magic wand. A hammer won't pound nails by itself, and

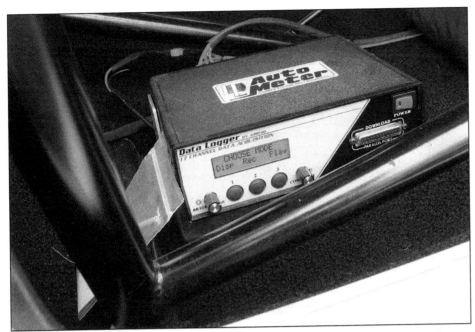

A data logger, or similar device, can monitor many of your vehicle's functions and provide valuable tuning information. Data loggers are permitted in most classes as long as they are programmed to collect information, and not adjust any of the vehicle's systems during a run.

mable shift light, so the tach provides a visual prompt for shifting the car at the designated RPM. This is a feature that helps the driver keep the revs in the heart of the powerband. Also, some tachs have an overrev lock, so the needle locks into position if the engine is overrevved. These tachs typically have four wires and can be quickly installed in most cars within a half an hour. The tachometer kit should contain complete instructions, mounting hardware, and necessary connectors.

Trans Brake

In the early days of drag racing, manual transmissions were used almost exclusively in almost every class, but that isn't the case anymore. While some of the faster cars such as Pro Stock, Pro Mod, and Comp Eliminator cars still use a clutch pedal and a manual shifter, automatic transmissions dominate almost every other form of drag racing, especially ET bracket racing. Early automatic transmissions and accompanying torque converters simply weren't strong enough to withstand the stress and strain of a drag-racing application. As technology has advanced, so has the strength and durability of automatic transmissions. Today, it is common to see automatic transmission-equipped race cars running in the low 6-second zone at well over 200 mph.

a delay box won't help make you a better racer unless you take the time to learn how to use it properly. In some cases, you can find all the information you need by simply reading the instructions, but there will also be times when you'll learn to use a product effectively through trial and error. As always, proper record keeping is necessary to take full advantage of the products that are available to you.

Aftermarket Tachometer

A stock or factory tachometer may be adequate for bracket racing, but an aftermarket tach will provide a wealth of information that a stock tach simply cannot deliver. An Auto Meter, Summit Racing, or other suitable aftermarket racing tachometer is a very important tool for extracting maximum performance from your car and posting consistent runs.

This racing tachometer clearly communicates engine RPM with its large 5-inch dial, and it features a programmable shift light, so you can shift at the ideal RPM.

These tachs make driving the car easier and feature a built-in recorder, so you can review a run, determine where you shifted, and see how the engine performed.

Aftermarket racing tachs are available in a large 5-inch diameter and can be mounted on the steering column, dash, A-pillar, and almost anywhere for quick reference. In addition, many contain a program-

One piece of equipment that has helped spur the grown of the automatic gearbox is the transmission brake, or trans brake for short. A trans brake is primarily an internally modified valve body that allows the transmission to engage first gear and reverse at the same time. The end result is that the engine can rev freely while the car does not move.

A transmission brake allows the transmission to engage first gear and reverse at the same time, so the driver can instantly transmit power to the rear tires simply by releasing a button. When the trans brake is released, it functions similar to the clutch on a manual transmission, instantly transmitting power through the driveline to rear tires. Trans-brake kits are available for most popular transmissions.

When the driver releases the trans brake, which is usually activated by a button on the steering wheel or shifter, reverse gear is no longer engaged, allowing the car to move forward. The effect is virtually identical to dumping the clutch pedal on a manually-shifted vehicle. A trans brake not only allows a racer to achieve quicker ETs by leaving the starting line at a higher RPM, it is also an effective way to fine-tune reaction times, especially when used in conjunction with a delay box.

Early trans brakes were relatively slow compared to today's units. They now release so quickly that just about every racer in Super Comp and Super Gas could red-light on a 4/10 pro tree if they didn't also use a delay box to slow their reaction times.

Line Lock

A line lock is a fairly simple device that allows a driver to lock the front wheels (or rear wheels in the case of a front-wheel-drive vehicle) while allowing the back tires to spin freely. A line lock is plumbed into the vehicle's braking system. Using an electric solenoid, the driver controls the front brakes by pushing a button, which is usually mounted on the shifter or steering wheel. In most cases, a driver will pump the brake pedal a few times to build pressure in the lines, and then engage the line lock, which holds the front wheels firmly in place. A line lock is especially useful for performing a stationary burnout, and many racers use it to hold their car on the starting line when staging. Once the burnout procedure is complete, most racers simply release the line-lock button, allowing the car to roll forward.

When used on the starting line, often in conjunction with a trans brake, the line lock is released as the car leaves the starting line. Although a line lock can be used in just about any vehicle, it is especially effective in manually shifted vehicles, such as Pro Stock cars, which may have a tendency to creep forward on the starting line when the clutch is engaged. If you watch Pro Stock drivers closely, most of them engage the line lock at the same time they are rolling in to stage, and in some cases, the front tires actually slide into the staging

A line lock uses an electric solenoid to hold the front brakes in place, so the racer can perform a burnout while stationary. Many racers use the line lock to hold the car in place on the starting line so RPM can be increased for a quick launch.

beams rather than roll. Staging a Pro Stock car is a complicated procedure that takes lots of practice, which is just one of the reasons why these drivers are considered to be some of the most talented in all of drag racing.

With the exception of most dragsters, which do not use front brakes, almost every other serious drag-racing vehicle will have a use for a line lock. If nothing else, a line lock can help make each burnout more consistent, heating the tires evenly from run to run, which will be a great asset when tuning your vehicle or trying to adjust your dial-in.

In almost every form of drag racing, a line lock is permitted. Even most of the lower levels of bracket racing, including so called "no electronics" classes, will permit competitors to use a line lock. In short, if your vehicle has even the slightest performance modifications, and it is going to see a drag strip more than just once or twice a year, then a line lock should probably be one of the first investments you make.

Two-Step and Three-Step Ignitions

A two- or three-step ignition, also known as a multi-stage rev limiter, temporarily interrupts the ignition signal to the engine, acting as a rev limiter. Typically, there are several ways to use a two-step rev limiter: on the starting line during the burnout, and as a high-end rev limiter. The burnout rev limiter is used to ensure the engine does not rev too high while a driver is doing a burnout. This can be especially useful in high-HP cars, which tend to rev very quickly and can damage valvesprings or other engine or driveline components if over-revved.

Used on the starting line, a two-step rev limiter can be a huge asset in the never-ending search for consistent reaction times. Basically, the two-step holds the car at a constant, preset RPM before each launch. This not only ensures that the car launches at the exact same RPM every time, but it also allows the driver to focus attention on the Christmas-tree lights instead of trying to manually hold the engine at a certain RPM.

Used in conjunction with a transmission brake or a line lock, the two-step is de-activated as soon as the driver releases the trans-brake or line-lock button, allowing the car to leave the starting line at full power. Early two-steps featured removable "chips" that featured adjustments in 100-rpm increments, but today's digital models are infinitely more adjustable, allowing a driver push-button control over the exact RPM as the car leaves the starting line.

The third and most widely used method of using a multi-stage ignition is a top-end rev limiter. Similar to the burnout rev limiter, the top-end limiter is used to protect the engine from excessive RPM. In the event of a transmission or driveshaft failure, a top-end rev limiter prevents the engine from "freewheeling." Without a high-rev limiter to interrupt the ignition circuit and keep the RPM to a reasonable level, the engine could very well over-rev, causing a lot of damage and possibly an accident.

Almost any racer can benefit from using a two-step ignition and some form of a two- or three-step, which are used by most bracket and NHRA-class racers. Just about every serious racer out there is using some form of a multi-stage rev limiter. In most cases, a two-step is a legal component since its primary function is to protect the engine from over-revving. The only exception might be a no-electronics bracket class.

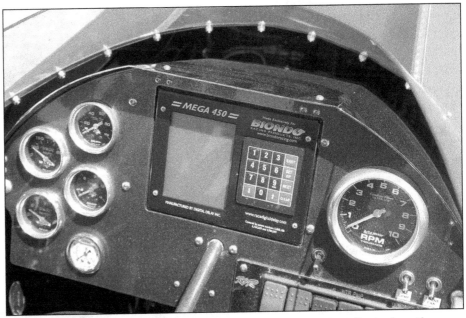

A delay box, such as the Biondo Mega 450, allows you to adjust when the car accelerates off the line. By adding or subtracting the amount of delay, the driver can respond to the first yellow light on a Christmas tree and achieve more consistent reaction times.

While rules vary greatly from track to track, most no-electronics classes prohibit the use of all electronic devices.

Delay Box

Have you ever wondered how some drivers can make run after run and have reaction times that are consistent within a few thousandths of a second? There are a handful of racers who have the natural ability to perform such a feat; but, more often than not, a delay box helps these drivers fine-tune their reaction times.

While a delay box can be beneficial when racing on both the full tree (three-amber countdown) and the pro tree, it is more beneficial when racing with a full tree. Early versions of delay boxes featured only a few hundredths of adjustment, allowing you to fine tune your reaction time when leaving off the last yellow light. By having 1 second (give or take a little) of delay, delay-box users then quickly figured out they could release the trans-brake button at the first hint of the first yellow light, essentially turning a full tree into a pro tree. It has been proven, both in theory and in real-life situations, that a driver will get more consistent reaction times when reacting to the first flash of light rather than sitting there and waiting for the flash of the third light.

A delay box simply allows you to control when the car leaves the starting line, thus allowing adjustment of your reaction times just by adding or subtracting the amount of delay that is programmed into the delay box. In bracket racing, drivers typically set their delay box so that they can release the trans-brake button as soon as the top yellow light comes on, even if that yellow light is in their opponent's lane. Even though drivers in Super Comp and Super Gas are leaving off a 4/10 pro tree, most of them also have the ability to red-light, so they typically add just a few hundredths of a second to their delay boxes, just enough to hit their target reaction time, which is usually somewhere in the 0.008 to 0.018 range. It might seem difficult to comprehend for someone who isn't familiar with bracket racing, but, yes, it is possible for a driver to adjust reaction times down to the thousandth of a second.

Most of the early delay boxes, which began to surface at ET racing events in the late 1970s and early 1980s, were simple devices that were little more than a timer that was wired into the trans-brake or line-lock switch. In fact, some of the earliest versions weren't adjustable. Today's delay boxes are highly sophisticated pieces of electronic equipment, which incorporate many features into the same unit. While basic function of the delay box is still to adjust reaction times, many other features have been added to further heighten the advantage of its use. Some of the state-of-the-art boxes allow you to bump down or tap up, or change the setting while the tree is counting down. If you feel like you were late or too early, there is the option to quickly hit a button, increasing or decreasing the amount of delay programmed into the delay box. In essence, this gives you another shot to fine tune your reaction time. Of course, the ability to quickly recognize a mistake and then react to it in the span of 2 seconds or less isn't something that I'd expect from a novice racer. Most drivers who use the bump-down/tap-up feature are experienced racers with hundreds and probably even thousands of runs under their belts. They're so familiar with their car and their own driving techniques that they instinctively know whether or not they got their intended reaction time before the car even moves.

If this sounds like it's getting high tech, it is. Other features incorporated into some of the newer delay boxes include shift activators, throttle stop and nitrous timers, digital tachometers with playback, and even a feature that allows you to practice your reaction times while sitting in the staging lanes.

In most of the faster bracket-racing classes, such as Super Pro, it is virtually impossible to be competitive

A delay box, such as the Biondo Mega 450, allows you to adjust when the car accelerates off the line. By adding or subtracting the amount of delay, the driver can respond to the first yellow light on a Christmas tree and achieve more consistent reaction times.

without the use of a delay box. The advantage of being able to react to the first yellow light is simply too great to overcome for all but the most gifted drivers.

To put all this information into perspective, imagine that you and a friend are racing and there is going to be a sequence of lights used to start the race. Now, think of how much easier it will be to take off as soon as you see the first light rather than waiting through a sequence of lights before moving. Leaving at the first hint of the first light eliminates the distraction factor that you'll likely encounter while watching each individual light count down.

When dealing with a thousandth of a second, which is often the difference between winning and losing, the slightest bit of distraction will almost certainly cost you the race. Besides the advantage of leaving off the "first flash" or in this case "top yellow," the other advantage is that you can easily make adjustments to the thousandth of a second. I'm not saying that a driver who doesn't use a delay box can't beat one that does, but any driver who aims for long-term success racing in a category that allows delay boxes would be wise to follow the crowd and use one.

As a side note, a delay box is easily one of the most controversial pieces of equipment ever to appear on a race car. Some drivers detest their very existence while some racers, especially those in the younger generation, have never raced without one. On more than one occasion, I've heard racers complain that delay boxes have "ruined sportsman racing." Some of the more vocal protesters argue that delay boxes have taken average racers and turned them into super stars and have reduced sportsman racing to a

crapshoot because virtually every driver is capable of achieving a nearly perfect reaction time run after run.

There is no doubt that the advent of delay boxes has done much to make sportsman and bracket racing an ultra-competitive

endeavor. As I noted at the beginning of this chapter, a delay box is nothing more than a tool, and if you don't use it effectively, you won't be a consistent winner.

To that end, they are not permitted in every class. In fact, under

A throttle stop, like the one pictured here, uses a timer and a solenoid to open and close the throttle at specified intervals. Throttle stops mechanically restrict both the air and fuel flow to the engine, usually by regulating the operation of the carburetor or fuel-injection system. Throttle stops are used primarily by Super-class racers, who are targeting a specific index but want to do so without sacrificing top-end performance.

By using a throttle stop, some Super Comp racers are able to take race cars that are capable of running in the low-7-sec range and consistently hit the 8.90 index while maintaining a 180-plus-mph top speed.

NHRA rules, they are only legal in the heads-up Super Comp, Super Gas, and Super Street categories and in certain bracket eliminators. They are strictly forbidden in eliminators such as Comp, Super Stock, and Stock. Any driver in one of those classes who is found with any sort of an adjustable delay box in their vehicle is subject to stiff penalties that can include a lengthy suspension.

Throttle Stops

Throttle stops are mechanical devices that allow a driver to intentionally slow their car down. They do so by restricting both the air and fuel flow to the engine, usually by controlling the operation of the carburetor or fuel-injection system. Most throttle stops are used in conjunction with a timer, allowing a driver to adjust not only the amount of air and fuel that go into the engine, but also the length of time that the engine is restricted. Actually, there are usually two timers; one to shut the throttle down, and another to open it back up.

Now, why in the world would any drag racer want to slow their car down? Well, with the advent of "Super class" racing, such as Super Comp, Super Gas, and Super Street, where drivers compete on a fixed index, it quickly became apparent that racers needed an effective way to adjust their ETs.

After all, a Super Gas car that could run the 9.90 index on a hot summer day in Las Vegas would almost certainly be much quicker on a cool spring day in almost any other part of the country. The fact is most of today's Super Gas cars are capable of running much quicker than the 9.90 index, and many of them are

quick enough to compete in Super Comp, where the index is a full second quicker. Likewise, many Super Comp cars are capable of running in the 7-second zone, legitimizing the need for a throttle stop.

Earlier models of throttle stops were very basic and all the adjustments were done mechanically. One popular unit was nothing more than a nut and bolt that limited the amount of travel in the carburetor linkage. Years later, racers and manufacturers realized that it would be much more consistent and reliable if they were somehow able to combine a throttle stop with a timer so that they could quickly and easily turn the throttle stop on and off.

Even sitting in the grandstands, it is very easy to spot a racer who is using a throttle stop. Typically, the car will launch at full power, and then quickly go silent. A couple of seconds later, the car will roar back to life and the driver will head for the finish line at full throttle. At first glance, it may appear that the car broke or the driver took his or her foot off the throttle; but it was just a carefully orchestrated exercise in attempting to hit the index.

Throttle stops are to Super-class racing what delay boxes are to bracket racing. I am sure you have heard the saying, "Don't bring a knife to a gun fight." Essentially the same thing applies here if you were to try to race in Super Comp, Super Gas, or Super Street without using a throttle stop. In short, no competitive racer would attempt to enter a major event without one. It's just too difficult to consistently hit the index.

By far, a throttle stop is most widely used in other sanctioning bodies super-class racing. A small percentage of racers use them on occasion when bracket racing and in other organizations. The legality of throttle stops varies and you should be sure to check it out from the sanctioning body and track you are running, but in most forms of racing that use a pre-set index, a throttle stop is permitted.

A side note: A funny moment regarding throttle stops occurred several years ago when Funny Car champion John Force was teaching his daughter, Ashley, to race a Super Comp car. Having never competed in anything other than a nitro-burning Funny Car, Force had no idea what a

Many racers launch their cars using a button mounted near the shifter or steering wheel that activates the transmission brake or line lock. In classes where a delay box is not permitted, some racers adjust their reaction times by using plastic shims to regulate the button travel.

throttle stop was or how it worked. On one of Ashley's first runs in her dragster, he watched as the car left the line and then coasted for a hundred feet or more before charging towards the finish line. Force later reprimanded his daughter, complaining that she "didn't have the guts to hold the throttle open for the whole run." Of course, the truth is that Ashley's state-of-the-art Super Comp car was equipped with a throttle stop and she was simply doing her best to get the car to run close to the 8.90-second index.

Weather Stations

Bob Dylan once sang, "You don't need a weatherman to know which way the wind blows," but there are times when you need to know how hard the wind is blowing. When fine tuning and predicting a vehicle's performance, it also helps to know things like air temperature, relative humidity, corrected altitude, and how strong the wind is blowing. It might seem a bit confusing at first, but fortunately you don't need to be a meteorologist to use a weather station.

A modern-day weather station will provide you with all of the important data when you simply turn it on. When using a weather station, it is highly recommended that you also keep a logbook or other detailed notes to catalog your findings. Once you build up a large library of data, you will quickly be able to reference your notes, researching how your car last performed under similar conditions.

Using the data gathered from a weather station, experienced racers can often predict their vehicle's ET to within a few thousandths of a second. This is no easy feat because a drastic change in weather can affect a car's performance by a half-second or more. There are plenty of documented cases of a racer arriving at the track too late to make a time-trial run, selecting a dial-in, and running within a few hundredths or even a few thousandths of that dial on the very first run. At first glance, it may seem like luck, but more often than not, that driver has used a weather station and referred to past logbooks

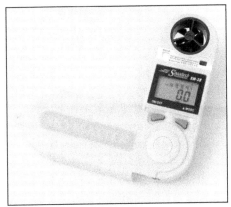

There are also a number of hand-held instruments on the market that will provide you with accurate weather-related data, which can be vital when setting up your car or choosing a dial-in.

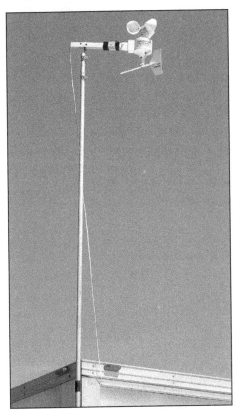

A weather station mounted to the top of your trailer can provide accurate information on a number of variables including temperature, relative humidity, wind speed, wind direction, and corrected altitude.

The current crop of highly advanced weather stations has a wireless feature that can send all pertinent data from your trailer to a pager, allowing you to make last-second adjustments prior to each run.

Even if you don't have a weather station, you can learn a lot about how wind speed and direction might affect your car's performance by watching various flags around the race track.

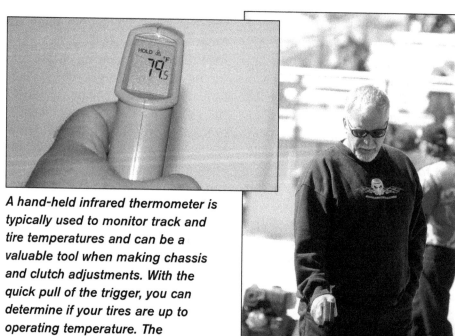

A hand-held infrared thermometer is typically used to monitor track and tire temperatures and can be a valuable tool when making chassis and clutch adjustments. With the quick pull of the trigger, you can determine if your tires are up to operating temperature. The thermometer allows you to keep track of these temperatures and much more so you analyze car performance at different temperatures.

in order to make an educated and precise prediction of what his or her vehicle should run. It's no different from cramming for a college exam; modern-day racers study when trying to tune and/or predict their vehicle's performance. The most common data gained from the use of a weather station is air temperature, humidity, barometric pressure, corrected altitude, vapor pressure, water grains, and wind direction and/or wind speed.

Once again, there are very few racers who can't benefit from tracking weather conditions. A weather station may seem like an unnecessary expenditure for a weekend hobby racer or someone who races a street-legal car, but the fact is that slower cars are usually less consistent than fast cars. Therefore, a quality weather station may actually be more useful to a sportsman racer.

Are weather stations legal? Of course they are. Since weather stations aren't physically attached to the race car, there are no rules whatsoever governing their use. The only exception would be if the data gathered by the weather station were somehow transmitted to the race car and adjustments, either made by the driver or done automatically, were made during a run. That sort of advanced technology, which does exist in other forms of motorsport, such as Formula 1, is prohibited in NHRA drag racing.

Infrared Thermometers

An infrared thermometer, more commonly known as a heat or temperature gun, is another tool racers use to tune and predict a car's performance. Just as changes in the air temperature will affect a car's performance, so do changes in the track temperature. Optimum track temperature can vary based on a number of factors including vehicle type, tire compound, and the amount of HP and torque your vehicle generates. As a general rule, a car will tend to spin the tires if the track temperature is excessively hot or excessively cold. Optimum performance is usually found somewhere in the middle; warm enough for the tires to work properly but not too hot so the surface gets greasy and slippery. An infrared thermometer will allow you to read track temperature and then make any necessary adjustments such as raising or lowering tire pressure.

Air and Electric Shifters

Air and electric shifters are yet other tools that aid in the consistency of the car's performance. Having an automatic shifter shift the car for you not only ensures a precise shift every time, but it also allows

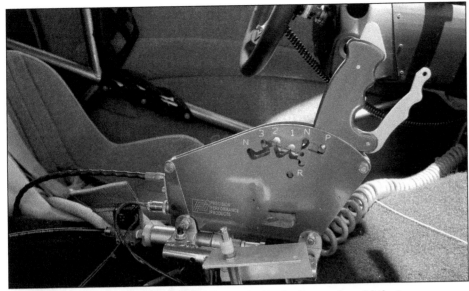

A typical air shifter uses compressed air to activate a solenoid that automatically shifts the transmission at a predetermined RPM level. By shifting at the same RPM on every pass, consistency is greatly improved, as there is less room for driver error.

A practice tree, which simulates the Christmas-tree starting system and measures a driver's reaction times, can be a valuable tool for helping to improve driver performance. This full-size Christmas tree replicates the drag strip experience and helps hone reaction times.

size Christmas tree complete with authentic LED lights.

A practice tree will provide your reaction time on each simulated pass, allowing you to fine tune your reaction times without ever setting foot in your race car. Most models will allow you to practice on a full or pro tree and you can usually adjust the roll out so you can accurately duplicate the launch of your particular vehicle.

Prediction Software

Years ago, tracking the changing air temperature throughout the day provided enough information to keep you competitive. As the level of competition heightened, the margin for error has shrunk considerably. Today, most bracket racers must consistently "split the atom," running within a hundredth or two of their dial-in on each pass. With the advent of weather stations, racers had the opportunity to measure humidity, barometric pressure, corrected altitude, and a number of other factors.

At the same time, prediction software began to appear. Prediction software is nothing more than a computer program that takes into account many different weather and track variables and compares these variables to your vehicle's past performance. On the surface, prediction software might seem like a good substitute for a logbook, but a better approach might be to use both and allow one to complement the other.

Putting It All Together

Now that you've read all of the above information on driving and tuning aids, you'll hopefully understand what it takes to be competitive

you to focus on the other details, such as car control. An automatic shifter can be programmed to shift at a predetermined RPM, or can be activated using a timer, a method favored by many Super-class racers.

Practice Trees

On a typical race weekend, you might get to make two or three time-trial runs, and then, with a bit of luck, you might make six or seven more runs during eliminations. Even if you race every weekend, that isn't a lot of track time in which to hone your driving skills. For this reason, most racers believe that practice trees are the best off-track tool a racer can have. A practice tree can come in various sizes but are all meant to simulate the starting-line system on the drag strip. Some typical variations of practice trees include small hand-held units that resemble a video game, while other more elaborate units feature a full-in today's technology-driven world. While all of the gadgets presented in this chapter are useful, it's sometimes difficult to imagine how they all work together. After all, with all of this equipment, you might wonder if you'd be too busy to actually drive the car. Since most operations are now automated, you actually have more time to concentrate on reaction time, keeping the car straight, judging the opponent at the finish line, and other aspects of driving.

In order to better understand driving aids, let's use a practical-application scenario. This case happens to be a typical quarter-mile run in an NHRA Super Gas car, which is equipped with a delay box, a throttle stop, an automated shifter, and a three-step rev limiter.

Once you've unloaded your Super Comp dragster and performed the routine safety check, you're ready for the first run of the weekend. After referring to logbooks from last year's event and checking the current conditions on the weather station, you have elected to maintain the current settings on your delay box, two-step, and throttle stop. After heading for the staging lanes, you will quickly check the condition and temperature of the starting line.

When you release the transbrake button, you leave the starting line at full power. One second into the run, the throttle stop activates, chopping the power. After coasting for exactly 1.25 seconds, you once again feel the sudden rush of acceleration as the throttle stop is deactivated. When the car is back under power the timer that controls the air-operated shifter does its thing, activating a solenoid that moves the shifter into high gear. Throughout all of this, you have never once had to move a hand off the steering wheel or shift focus from the rapidly approaching finish line.

After making your first run, you can now begin to make adjustments in order to prepare for the next run. If the car is too fast or too slow, a quick adjustment of the throttle-stop timers will correct the problem. If you red-lighted, you will likely want to add some time to the delay box. If

The hand-held device also simulates the Christmas-tree starting system and allows the drag racer to practice almost anywhere.

Used properly, delay boxes, throttle stops, air shifters, practice trees, and other devices can be helpful. It often takes time and practice to learn how to effectively use these devices and get them dialed in on a particular car. While these driver aids can help improve consistency and performance, success or failure is largely dependent on the driver and crew.

the tires could be felt spinning on the starting line, you might also adjust the two-step to lower the starting-line RPM before making the next run.

If all goes according to plan, you will be very "dialed-in" by the time you get to eliminations, formulating a game plan that includes a competitive reaction time and a car that is going to run the exact ET that is expected. Now, all that remains is for you to execute your game plan, performing a consistent burnout, releasing the trans-brake button on time, and properly judging the opponent as the finish line approaches. Now that wasn't too difficult, was it?

A data-acquisition system can monitor a variety of the functions of a race car including tire and/or driveline slippage, wheel speed, exhaust temperatures, and shift points. After each run, the information is downloaded from the vehicle to a computer for analysis. Data acquisition is particularly useful for identifying areas in which the driver can improve. Because everything happens so fast during the run, it's virtually impossible for the driver to be a reliable data acquisition system. A successful racer should keep a running database of all the runs and examine it for improving performance—the professional race teams do.

Electrical problems can be some of the most difficult problems to diagnose and repair, especially when you're trying to race. When it comes to wiring, the best advice is to keep it as simple as possible. To that end, an aftermarket wiring kit can be a big help.

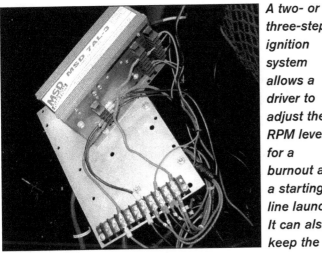

A two- or three-step ignition system allows a driver to adjust the RPM level for a burnout and a starting-line launch. It can also keep the engine from over-revving in the event of a driveline failure.

A Super Comp dragster cockpit with the cowl removed reveals a digital ignition system (the large gold box), an on-board data recorder (the small black box) and a small air tank used to activate the air shifter solenoid. The on-board data recorder is plugged into a laptop after each run, and the information is downloaded so it can be closely analyzed and evaluated.

THE BASICS OF BRACKET RACING

After reading this far, you have no doubt noticed that much of the content of this book revolves around bracket racing; there's a good reason for that. Although other forms of racing have gained tremendous popularity in recent years, including NHRA street-legal races, NHRA class racing, and drag racing put on by other sanctioning bodies, the majority of all the drag-racing activity conducted across North America is still in the form of bracket or handicap-style racing. What many do not know, however, is just how and why ET bracket racing began and how it got to be so popular.

In the early 1960s, Lions Dragstrip just outside of Long Beach, California, was perhaps the most famous drag strip in the world. Known throughout the country for its weekly nitro shows and the cool ocean breeze that often produced record-setting performances, Lions, which closed in late 1972, is also the place where future stars such as Don "the Snake" Prudhomme, James Warren, and a host of others launched their careers. A somewhat lesser-known fact is that Lions was also the birthplace of what is today known as bracket racing.

As early as 1962, the management at Lions, led by drag-racing pioneer C.J. "Pappy" Hart, launched a program where vehicles competed heads-up in 1-second classes ranging from 9 seconds to 20 seconds. The rules were relatively simple. For example, if you raced in the 13-second class and ran a 12.99, then you lost, even if a competitor crossed the finish line first. It was then said that competitor "broke out" of that 1-second time bracket. Hence the terms breakout and bracket were established, which are in very familiar usage today.

The breakout rule was a new concept, but one that was necessary in order to stem the rising cost of racing and place more importance on driver skill and consistency. The rule also

During the advent of ET bracket racing in the 1960s, competitors were handicapped according to a dial-in, which helped pave the way for Super-class racing. Drivers in this class race on a fixed 8.90-, 9.90-, or 10.90-second index.

prevented particular individuals from dominating traditional class racing, which had been the mainstay of organized competition since the early 1950s. With the breakout rule in effect, competitors could simply choose a class that fit their particular vehicle as well as their budget. Enforcing breakouts also added an additional element of driver skill to the mix; finish-line driving. No longer able to concentrate solely on reaction times, drivers quickly figured out that the key to success in bracket racing was to win by the smallest amount possible, making it necessary for them to properly "judge" their opponent as the finish line approached.

Interestingly enough, the early Lions heads-up brackets did not utilize a handicap start because the timing systems of the day did not have the capability to stagger each lane's starting-line light sequence. It should also be noted that, prior to the introduction of the "Christmas" starting lights tree, many tracks conducted rudimentary forms of handicap racing by physically placing the slower car farther down the track, usually by the standard of a 1/2 second per car length.

In fact, many of the old tracks had painted hash marks, usually about 20 to 25 feet apart, located on the shoulders where the slower car was staged. Haphazard handicap racing was likely conducted elsewhere prior to the Lions program by simply giving a slower car a head start from the flagman, which no doubt created many problems. Competitors could easily find grounds to complain about everything from their opponent jumping the gun to the starter giving one competitor an unfair advantage over the other.

Ultimately, the Lions bracket program proved to be a huge success, providing an exciting new alternative to traditional class racing. It's hardly a surprise that it was quickly adopted by other racetracks across the country. By the late 1970s, bracket racing had proved to be a needed shot in the arm for track promoters. The poor economy of the era had already decimated the attendance of legal-class cars to the point that many tracks simply closed.

The rapidly growing popularity of bracket racing proved to be a savior for many track promoters because formerly shrinking entry lists began to increase. The success of bracket racing was not only measured by the influx of new customers, but in the number of old class cars that were resurrected as bracket machines because they could once again be competitive. By 1980, only a handful of tracks offered any weekly class-racing program at all. By the end of the 1981 season, NHRA followed suit, doing away with the popular Modified Eliminator and making

way for the latest craze, Super Gas. Today, traditional class racing events for competitors in Comp, Modified, Super Stock, and Stock are limited to NHRA national, divisional, and other special events.

As a side note, the evolution of ET bracket racing eventually led to what is today known as Super Class racing. Super Class is formed by the popular NHRA eliminators known as Super Comp, Super Gas, and Super Street, which feature fixed indexes of 8.90, 9.90, and 10.90, respectively. Today, these classes are hugely popular with most major events drawing upwards of 100 participants.

The origins of these classes can be traced to the original program at Lions, but more accurately, they were a spin-off of the Pro Gas class that was created in Redding, California, in 1976. Designed to give Gas Coupe racers a place to compete without spending a fortune to remain competitive, the Pro Gas class featured a common 9.50-second index, and the breakout rule was enforced. Pro Gas events proved to be highly successful

No matter where you race or what type of vehicle your drive, it's important that your car number and class are clearly visible so that workers in the timing tower can accurately keep track of each race. Your dial-in needs to be clearly posted, as well.

as the heads-up starts and 9-second performances proved to be a hit with the racers and the fans.

A similar Pro Gas movement started in northeastern Ohio in 1978 on a 9.90 index. The old American Hot Rod Association adopted those rules to create a Pro Gas Eliminator at AHRA National events in 1979. In subsequent years, they added Modified Gas Eliminator (10.90 index) and a Super Comp Eliminator (7.90 index). In 1980, the NHRA followed suit, offering Pro Gas on a 9.80 index (not 9.90). Within three years, NHRA had revised the index to 9.90 and added 8.90 and 10.90 classes, as well.

As is often the case with historically significant events, there is certainly some debate about the origins of bracket/handicap racing. While it's possible that some enterprising track operator created a similar version of bracket racing prior to the 1962 Lions series, it isn't as well documented and certainly wasn't as popular or successful as the events held at Lions. Although there have been some minor format tweaks over the years, bracket racing remains much the same as it was in the early days. It remains an effective way to equalize competition among sportsman racers, helping to keep a level playing field for all.

The Current State of Bracket Racing

It might be stating the obvious, but bracket racing has come a long way since the early days of Lions Dragstrip. This is especially true when it comes to performance. Early bracket cars rarely ran quicker than 10 seconds on a quarter-mile, a far cry from today, where a typical gas-powered dragster can easily run in

the low-7-second zone at speeds of over 175 mph. This performance is comparable to a mid-1960s Top Fuel dragster. Furthermore, most of today's vehicles require a fraction of the maintenance needed by their predecessors. It is common for a bracket racer to go a full season, encompassing as many as 500 runs, without performing anything other than routine maintenance thanks to advances in tire, transmission, and engine technology.

Consistency is another hallmark of current bracket racers. Years ago, any racer who could make five or six runs within 1/10 second had a great chance to achieve success in bracket racing. Today, in classes that permit the use of electronics such as delay boxes and two-step ignition systems, packages of 0.030 second are routine. It is also common for racers to flirt with perfection, putting together a string of eight or nine runs with reaction times ranging from 0.000 to 0.020 and ETs that exhibit similar consistency.

Naturally, in those classes that do not permit the use of delay boxes or other electronic aids, the window of

opportunity is much greater, meaning that reaction times are generally not as close to perfect and many of the cars that compete in those classes are not as consistent. This means that even a racer with a moderate amount of skill has a chance to be successful.

To help understand just how often modern-day bracket racers are capable of splitting the atom, one need look no further than the "run for the money" program that is featured at many large ET events. As part of the program, racers select a dial-in for a time-trial run and then shoot for the best package, combining their starting-line reaction time with their ET against the dial-in. The best package of the race earns a bonus and in most big events the winning package is often within a few thousandths of a second of perfect.

While it's true that the sport's best bracket racers are capable of turning in consistent performances from run to run, their prowess should not discourage you from becoming a bracket racer. I don't want you to think that you have to be an expert racer with a perfect race car to be successful and enjoy the sport because

With performances in the mid-7-second range and relatively low maintenance costs, the dragsters of today's ET bracket racers are a far cry from the vehicles that raced during bracket racing's infancy.

that simply isn't the case. Even the best racers make occasional mistakes such as red lighting and breaking out, and if you continually work towards bettering your driving skills and improving the consistency of your car, you will almost certainly be successful regardless of the level of competition you're facing.

It's well documented that much of the appeal of bracket racing stems from the fact that on any given day, one racer can easily beat another regardless of their level of talent or experience. To explain it another way, if you're a novice golfer and could somehow play 100 rounds against Tiger Woods, you'd probably never beat him even once because his skill advantage is simply too great to overcome. That's not the case in bracket racing, for the simple reason that if you have a perfect reaction time and match your dial-in, you cannot be beaten regardless of who your opponent is and what he or she does. Of course, putting together a perfect run is much easier said than done, but the final point to make here is that as you continually whittle away at your reaction times and continuously learn how to dial your vehicle correctly, you'll ultimately win more races.

ET bracket racing was created to promote fair competition between vehicles of varying performance levels, and that still holds true today. Bracket racing's loose class structure and liberal rules make it possible for street-legal cars to compete successfully against all-out race cars.

In bracket racing, all-out performance takes a back seat to consistency. Most experienced bracket racers have finely honed car performance, set-ups, launching procedure, and driving technique, so it's common to see a good bracket racer make eight or nine runs within a few hundredths of one another.

Bracket Racing Versus Other Forms of Drag Racing

First off, I will shed some light on an often-misunderstood aspect of bracket racing. There is a certain segment of the drag-racing fraternity that feels that bracket racing is somehow beneath them or that bracket racers aren't real racers. Their disdain for the event apparently stems from the use of the breakout rule. While it's entirely understandable that some might frown upon the notion of not racing full-throttle to the finish line in order to win a race, it could easily be argued that, due to the added element of finish-line driving, and the ultra-competitive environment, that it might actually be harder to be a consistent winner in bracket racing than in other forms of drag racing. To be perfectly blunt about it, some of the most successful bracket racers are also some of drag racing's best drivers and would almost certainly succeed at drag racing's highest levels, including the professional classes, if given the opportunity.

Another common misconception regarding bracket racing is that competitors are merely attempting to match their dial-in time in order to win the race. The fact is that bracket racers, like virtually everyone else who chooses to drag race, make every effort to cross the finish line ahead of their opponent. While it's certainly true that drivers can and often do win bracket races by hitting the brakes or lifting off the throttle and letting their opponents finish first, that is almost never the primary objective. Lifting, then hitting the brakes, or "dumping" as it is often called, is a technique employed only when circumstances dictate that it is the best available option. In most cases, it's not the primary goal.

While I'm dispelling myths, I can also eliminate another one regarding bracket racing. The long-held notion that bracket racers don't worry about the performance of their vehicles is also untrue. While bracket racers don't need to search for every possible bit of HP available, attention to every aspect of the operation of their vehicles is mandatory. As part of the never-ending search for improved consistency, bracket racers experiment, tinker, and fine tune their cars every bit as much as their class-racing counterparts. It's common for bracket racers to try several different transmissions, torque converters, carburetors, camshafts, and other components in an effort to find the one that best suits their needs. To be sure, modern bracket cars are much more sophisticated and refined than their predecessors; in fact, most of them are purpose-built for bracket racing.

The only real major difference between bracket racing and traditional NHRA or other class-legal racing is that a bracket car is almost never pushed to the limits of its performance. With the possible exception of some bracket classes that feature a qualified field, such as Quick 32, Top Comp, or Top Dragster, there is little incentive for bracket racers to extract every last ounce of performance from their race cars. Ironically, competitors in Super Stock and Stock often take the same approach, using a conservative tune-up whenever necessary and seeking all-out performance only in qualifying or during a heads-up run against an opponent in the same class, as the breakout rule is not

Driver skill, including the ability to produce competitive reaction times and properly judge opponents at the finish line, is often the difference between winning and just running in ET bracket racing.

These days, most ET bracket racers are highly skilled and capable of achieving competitive reaction times on a consistent basis. That helps explain why many races are decided by just a few feet or less at the finish line.

enforced during those races. As noted earlier, most early bracket vehicles were simply displaced class cars that were no longer competitive in Modified, Comp, Super Stock, or Stock Eliminator. Conversely, most of today's class cars do most of their racing in a bracket-style format.

Bracket racing was created with the intention of giving everyone a fair shot at victory and as I've noted, that still holds true today. A properly built bracket car should easily satisfy almost anyone's need for speed and should also challenge mechanical and driving abilities. While some racers will never fully warm to the idea of bracket racing, they are a minority since over the past three decades, bracket racing has become a universally accepted form of legitimate competition. At any rate, one of the great things about drag racing is the opportunity for every competitor to pick and choose the type of vehicle they race and the format in which they choose to race it.

Understanding Reaction Time

By definition, reaction time is the electronically clocked measurement of a driver's response to the lights on the Christmas tree. Your reaction time, which is included as part of the information printed on your time slip, is measured from the flash of the last amber light on the Christmas tree, or the flash of all three lights in the case of a pro tree, and the point at which the vehicle actually accelerates out of the starting line stage beams. Although considered the true measurement of a driver's reflexes, it also gauges the responsiveness of the vehicle's engine and chassis. A reaction time of 0.000 second is considered perfect, meaning that the

driver's front wheels left the starting line at the exact moment (within a thousandth of a second) that the green light flashed. Foul starts, or red lights, are expressed as a negative value. For example, a driver who received a 0.002 reaction time moved from the starting line two-thousandths of a second before the green starting light illuminated.

Reaction time, which is a measure of a driver's response to the Christmas-tree starting lines, is a critical element of bracket racing. A driver's goal is to leave the starting line at the same instant the green light comes on. To do this, a driver starts to launch the car when the last amber light on the Christmas tree flashes. A 4/10 and 5/10 amber tree allows gives you 0.400 or 0.500 second, respectively, between the last amber light and green light. The closer your reaction time is to 0.400 or 0.500 second, the better the run. However, if your car leaves the line faster than 0.400 or 0.500 second, you have red-lighted and you're disqualified.

In cars equipped with a delay box, it's possible for a driver to react to the first flash of yellow light, and then have the car leave the starting line a couple of seconds later. A reaction time of 0.000-second is considered perfect.

When you have a better reaction time than your opponent you're said to have gotten a "holeshot," which means that it is possible to reach the finish line first, even if you run a slower ET than your opponent. For example, a driver who cuts a perfect 0.000 reaction time and runs a 10.00-second ET will cross the finish line before an opponent who has a 0.085 reaction time and runs a 9.95 ET. Yes, the first driver ran slower but finished first because of superior starting-line reaction time.

If the concept of reaction time and holeshots is still a bit confusing, think of it this way: If you are involved in a 100-meter dash against an Olympic sprinter, you probably have no chance to win. However, if you left the starting blocks as soon as the starter's pistol fired and the Olympic sprinter stayed on the starting line for 3 to 4 seconds, you'd easily get to the finish first, even though your opponent's ET would be much quicker than yours. The same principle applies to reaction time and drag racing. As always, it's important to remember that the clocks on a drag strip don't start when the light turns green, but rather when the vehicle actually leaves the starting line. That's a concept that many novice racers don't always grasp immediately, but it's an important one to fully comprehend.

Getting off the starting line ahead of your opponent will allow you to win a lot of races, and it is quite honestly what separates a great racer from an average one. Obviously, reaction time is a critical element for any drag racer from Top Fuel to Stock Eliminator. Unlike other forms of racing, where HP can often help to overcome a slow start, the ability to have consistently quick reaction times is essential for long-term success in bracket racing. Since you can't overpower your opponents you've got to outdrive them, and that means continuously refining your driving technique and tuning your vehicle in order to achieve the best possible reaction times.

As a first-time or novice racer, your reaction times are likely to vary by a wide margin due, at least, to your lack of experience. Obviously, it takes focus and concentration in order to achieve competitive reaction times, and as you make more runs, you'll figure out which techniques work and which ones do not. In most cases, the simple ability to block

A driver who gains a significant reaction-time advantage over an opponent and leaves the line first gets the "holeshot." This makes it possible for him or her to win even if his or her ET is slower than his or her opponent's time.

When it comes to reaction times, most experienced racers instinctively know which techniques work and which ones don't. Novice drivers can usually figure it out with a little experience, but in most cases, it takes practice and some experience to find a launching technique that is effective and suits your individual taste.

outside distractions including noises, lights, and movements, will go a long way towards helping to improve your reaction times. Having a consistent vehicle is also vital to achieving competitive reaction times.

Most veteran racers don't need to see their time slip to know whether they've had a good reaction time or a bad one. Their instincts are so keen that they can usually predict their reaction time, usually within a hundredth or two, as soon as they leave the starting line. With a bit of experience, just about any racer will be able to make a similar determination, knowing where they stand long before they've seen the results on their time slip. In upcoming chapters, I'll provide a more in-depth look at reaction times and explain some detailed strategies for "cutting lights" as close to perfect as possible.

Dial-Ins and Breakouts

As I've noted in my quick review of bracket-racing history, when the electronic Christmas-tree starting system and its accompanying handicap-start capabilities became available around 1964, tracks could offer competitors the opportunity to choose, or dial in, their own index in 0.01-second increments, creating

When bracket racing at night, the Christmas tree lights will appear brighter than during the daytime and your reaction times will improve, so you'll need to make adjustments either to your vehicle or to your delay box in order to keep from red-lighting.

Here is a prime example of how a driver might lose his concentration on the starting line. Note that as the Christmas tree is counting down, the vehicle in the other lane is right in this driver's line of sight, momentarily distracting him and leading to a red-light start.

In bracket racing, the driver with the slower dial-in is afforded a head start against a faster opponent.

their own time-bracket parameters. As an interesting side note, each competitor's handicap was entered into the original Chrondek handicapping computer by way of thumbwheel dials, which explains the origin of the term "dial in."

A dial-in is simply an ET, selected by a competitor, which is a prediction of what the racer expects his or her vehicle to run. In a bracket race, a dial-in is used to establish a handicap. As an example, if competitor A has selected a dial-in of 10.00 seconds, and competitor B has chosen a dial-in of 10.50 seconds, then competitor B will receive a 1/2-second (.50-second) handicap start, meaning simply that the countdown sequence of lights on side B of the Christmas tree will begin one half-second before competitor A's tree begins.

A breakout is simply when a competitor's ET exceeds his or her dial-in time. For example, on a dial-in of 10.00 seconds, a competitor

who runs a 9.99 has committed a breakout and will lose, even if he or she crosses the finish line before the opponent. But what happens if both competitors break out? That occurrence, which is termed a double breakout, happens frequently. In that case, the driver who is under his or her dial-in by the least amount is the winner. So, if driver A should happen to run a 9.95 on a 10.00 dial-in and driver B runs a 10.41 on his or her 10.47 dial-in, then driver A will win the race because he or she ran under their dial by a smaller amount (0.050 second for driver A versus 0.060 second for driver B, a difference of 0.010 second). As noted earlier, dial-ins and breakouts are critical elements of bracket racing, which help to differentiate it from other forms of drag-racing competition.

If you haven't figured it out by now, I'll emphasize the point by once again noting that, along with reaction time, choosing the correct

dial-in is one of the most crucially important elements for success in bracket racing. In upcoming chapters, you'll learn exactly how to do just that.

Why Should I Bracket Race?

A better question might be, why shouldn't you bracket race? It is a challenging, relatively affordable, and above all fun way to get involved in drag racing. In fact, bracket racing might just be the most cost-effective form of motorsports there is, which probably goes a long way towards explaining its ever-increasing popularity. The professional racers you see racing at national events each weekend on television represent just a tiny fraction of the thousands of racers who compete at the nation's drag strips each week.

There are currently about 150 to 200 drag strips operating across North America and most of them offer some sort of regular bracket-racing series where competitors can compete for points and money on a weekly basis. Points-based programs that culminate in the crowning of track champions at the end of the season are also popular. This gives local racers the opportunity to compete for a championship without having to travel long distances or incur the expense of racing on national level.

If you're still not convinced and are looking for another good reason to begin bracket racing, I can provide you with all the motivation you should need in a single word: money. Since the mid-1970s, drag-racing promoters have figured out that one of the best ways to attract large numbers of ET bracket racers is

At most ET bracket racing events, the finish line scoreboards display the dial-in time of each competitor prior to each race. It's always a good idea to check the scoreboards before staging to make sure your dial-in is correct. If it's incorrect, you need to notify someone in scoring, so your dial-in is correctly shown.

to post large and in some cases outrageous purses for the winners. Some of the richest events in drag racing are bracket races, with the winners often earning more money in a single weekend than the average worker makes in several months.

Today, if you're an ET bracket racer competing in the Super Pro division, you likely won't have to travel far to race for $10,000 to $20,000 or more on a given weekend. Likewise, a small entry fee can often reap sizable rewards even with an unmodified street-driven car. Throughout the USA, there are several major events designed specifically for footbrake or non-electronics cars that routinely pay upwards of $5,000 to $10,000 or more to the winner.

The most extreme example of "dialing for dollars" is the annual Million Dollar Drag Race held each fall at Memphis Motorsports Park. The Million Dollar Drag Race features a hefty $2,000 entry fee, but top payouts are potentially life changing. Since its inception in 1997, the champion of the Million Dollar race has received $175,000 to $325,000, and the payout could potentially reach $1 million if the event attracts 500 competitors.

One of the most successful bracket-racing programs in history

In this typically close bracket race, the competitor in the left lane ran a 9.389 on his 9.36 dial-in for the win, while his right-lane opponent ran a 9.359 on his 9.32 dial-in. Often, bracket races are decided by narrower margins, and an experienced driver has a good feel for posting an ET close to the dial-in time without breaking out.

While most racers compete for the love of the sport, it's also possible to earn a big paycheck in bracket racing events. Some of the biggest races in the country feature life-changing rewards for the winners.

is the NHRA Summit ET Racing Series. Launched in 2000, the NHRA Summit Racing Series is a great program that allows bracket competitors to compete for an NHRA national championship. The program begins at local member tracks where racers compete each week for the right to compete in one of the seven Summit Racing Series divisional championships, which are held annually in each of NHRA's seven geographic regions.

Each Summit Racing Series divisional event features four different classes of competition: Super Pro, Pro, Sportsman, and Motorcycle, which are designed to accommodate racers in a wide variety of vehicles and skill levels. The 28 individual winners of each Summit divisional event receive an invitation to the annual Automobile Club of Southern California NHRA Finals in Pomona, California, where they race for a national championship and a large cash bonus.

While there are only a select few with the resources and talent to bracket race as a full-time profession, it is certainly possible for even a part-time racer to turn a profit, or at the very least offset some operating expenses, by competing in some of the sport's bigger events.

Most novice racers should avoid running a highly modified and higher-maintenance car. They should concentrate on developing competitive driving skills, rather than being concerned with car performance and reliability. Most stock or mildly modified ET bracket cars require a minimal amount of maintenance in order to run consistently week after week.

Other than stringent safety requirements, there are few rules in bracket racing, so you're almost guaranteed to "run what you brung." In turn, racers are allowed to build and race just about any vehicle. The only limit is your imagination.

The NHRA "Wally" trophy, named for late National Hot Rod Association founder Wally Parks, is the trophy that is most coveted by drag racers.

ADVANCED BRACKET RACING STRATEGY

If you've read each chapter of this book and, more importantly, if you've actually gone to your local track and participated in a few races, you should fully understand the fundamental elements of drag racing. You should have a firm grasp of how the Christmas tree works and how the timing system accurately measures each race. You should also have begun to establish a driving routine that enables you to make clean, fast runs. In addition, you should by now

have honed your starting-line skills so that your reaction times are competitive. So, now that you've accomplished all that, what's left? The answer to that is simple. It's time to start winning. Drag racing school instructor Frank Hawley has often maintained, "Driving a race car is fun, but the real thrill comes from winning." Of course, Hawley's assessment is completely correct, and anyone who has ever experienced the thrill of victory will agree with him.

This chapter covers the fundamental elements that all successful bracket racers should master: reaction times, ETs, choosing a proper dial-in, and driving the finish line.

Posting Consistent Reaction Times

As we've noted several times already, it doesn't matter whether you drive a Top Fuel dragster or the family sedan, you aren't going to have any level of success unless you master the art of achieving reaction times that are both consistent and quick.

Obviously, there are a number of factors that must be considered when determining the best way to cut consistently quick lights. The technique differs greatly when racing on a full tree as opposed to a pro tree, and if your particular application permits the use of a driving aid such as a delay box, that introduces an additional element into the equation. Although, when used properly, a driving aid will undoubtedly help you in your quest for short reaction times.

Once you've grasped the essence of bracket racing, your goal should be to improve your reaction times and make your ETs more consistent.

No matter what type of racing you do, the first thing to know is that your staging process must be consistent on every run. As you're moving your vehicle into the staging lights, you must move forward slowly so that your car is in the same position on each and every run. This is extremely critical because a slight difference in staging, even as little as a half-inch, can have a dramatic effect on both your reaction time and your ET. In many cases, rolling too far forward will affect your reaction time to the point where a competitive green light will turn into a painful red light. At the same time, staging deeper than expected will slow your ET, possibly by 1/10 second or more, so even if you don't red-light, you might lose the race because you ran too far over your dial-in.

Consistent staging isn't difficult, but it does require a bit of practice. Some drivers, even those with years of experience behind the wheel, often look cumbersome when staging. They furiously pump the brake pedal, causing the front end of their car to bob up and down. Others will have their engine RPM too high, making it difficult to roll forward in small increments. A proper staging technique should be smooth and fluid, with the vehicle slowly rolling forward just enough to illuminate the second yellow stage light.

One you've learned to stage your car in the same spot, you'll want to monitor and control your engine RPM so that your car will react the same way each time. If you normally leave the starting line with the engine at 1,500 rpm and then suddenly start leaving at 2,000 rpm, it will affect both reaction time and ET. You might recall that many drivers, especially those who aren't allowed to use delay boxes, use engine RPM to adjust their reaction times. When you find a launch RPM that works for you, it's important that you're able to duplicate it run after run.

When it comes to your vehicle and reaction times, RPM isn't the only determining factor. Engine heat, tire pressure and temperature, driveline slack, and converter slippage will all affect your lights, which is why it's important to know your vehicle inside and out. Ideally, you want to race a vehicle that is consistent from run to run. As a driver, you will be a variable when it comes to reaction times, so it important that your vehicle be consistent. That way, if you're having difficulty hitting your target reaction time, you won't have to wonder if the problem is you or your car.

What should be going through your mind when you light the second stage bulb and prepare for a race? In a word: nothing. That's right; your mind should be completely blank. Leaving the starting line is simply a reaction to a stimulus, which in this case, happens to be a yellow light. Thinking about anything else is just a distraction that will adversely affect your reaction time. Racing on a full tree, some drivers attempt to count down along with each light as they come on, shifting their attention from the first to the second to the third yellow light, and then hitting the gas pedal as soon as it comes on. Some racers are able to use this tactic successfully but most simply focus their attention on the last amber light and pay no attention whatsoever to the first two. It takes a bit of practice to not be distracted by the glow of the first two lights, but after a few runs, most people are able to get the hang of it.

Sometimes, it's also hard not to be distracted by your surroundings. On the starting line, everything—your opponent, photographers, the noise of your or your opponent's

In order to maintain consistent reaction times, it's important to stage the exact same way every time you make a run. Even a small variation in your staging process can have a big affect on your ETs and speeds.

Tire pressure, both front and rear, can affect reaction times as well as ETs so it's important that it be checked often. Many racers use tire-pressure adjustments to adjust their reaction times, especially in classes where delay boxes aren't permitted.

The search for consistent ETs begins with a properly built race car. After your first few weekends of racing, you should gain the knowledge and experience necessary to run consistently. The tires, transmission, chassis, suspension, and other components should all be built to handle the HP that's under the hood.

The ability to eliminate outside distractions goes a long way towards helping your reaction times. Successful professional racers have a routine for preparing to race. When the belts are fastened and the gloves on, the driver has a plan to peak concentration on the line. When you stage, your sole focus should be on the Christmas-tree lights.

engine, or even fans in the stands—can be a potential distraction. The driver who is best able to block out those distractions will have a distinct advantage over one who can't. In some cases, if you are bracket racing and your opponent is receiving a head start, his or her car will be in your line of vision just as your side of the Christmas tree is counting down. Imagine that your opponent is getting a head start of 1.5 seconds against you and is driving a yellow car. Now imagine trying to focus on a single amber-colored light bulb while your opponent's car is directly in your line of sight. It takes a fair amount of discipline to keep your composure in a situation like that, but it isn't impossible. You just have to maintain your focus.

One starting-line tactic that is used successfully by many racers is known as "blocking," which is nothing more than a crude but effective method of turning a full tree into a pro tree by blocking out the first and second yellow lights on the Christmas tree. Some drivers block the first two lights by strategically positioning their car's visor so that nothing is visible except the last yellow lights. Others will simply hold their hand in front of their face or close one eye so that they can't see anything but the last yellow light. Whatever the method, the end result is the same as racing on a pro tree, meaning that they can leave at the first hint of a yellow light instead of waiting for each light to count down individually. An additional benefit of blocking is that it helps reduce the risk of red lights because drivers who block don't anticipate the last yellow light as much. The downside of blocking is that it isn't as effective at night since the glow of the first two yellow lights is often distracting, although many successful racers use this method even when night racing.

When it comes to reaction times, practice is the key and fortunately there are plenty of devices that can help you hone your skills. For many racers, a practice tree is one of the smartest investments. Whether it's a small battery-operated unit that fits in the palm of your hand or a full-size authentic national-event-style Christmas tree that fits in your garage or living room, a practice tree will give you the ability to simulate any desired number of runs without burning a drop of fuel in your race car. By using a practice tree, you not only familiarize yourself with the starting-line lights, but you can also monitor how you react to them. Do your reaction times get slower after eating a big meal? Do you tend to get quicker as the sun goes down? Spending a few hours or even a few minutes on a practice tree will give you the answers to these and a host of other questions regarding reaction time.

As an interesting side note, prior to about 1985, the Christmas tree featured a five-amber-light sequence instead of the three amber lights that are commonplace today. That meant that a driver racing on a full tree needed to hold his or her concentration for 2.5 seconds before leaving the line. While 2.5 seconds might not sound like much time, it can seem like an eternity when you're trying to focus all of your attention on a single light bulb. It's no surprise that many drivers got antsy and either red-lighted or were late leaving the line. It also might be no surprise that the current three-amber tree was welcomed with open arms by most competitors.

Making Your Car Consistent

If your reaction times or ETs are not consistent, the first question you should ask yourself is, "Is it me or my car?" If you're convinced that you are driving the car the same way each time—staging the same, leaving at the same RPM, shifting at the right time—and your time slips rarely match, then you'll probably want to take a closer look at your vehicle.

Obviously, the fewer number of variables in any system, the simpler it will be. When driven properly, most vehicles are consistent, but it should be obvious that a dragster with a solid-mounted rear end will likely be much more consistent than a street car simply because the dragster doesn't have a suspension. This is at least one less variable than its street-going counterpart. No matter what vehicle you choose to race, you've got to first make sure it doesn't spin the tires. In bracket racing, performance isn't an issue, and most racers use a bigger tire than is really necessary because they don't want to worry about tire spin. Running a big tire in conjunction with a torque converter that is excessively loose can make for an extremely inconsistent race car.

Common sense should tell you that a radical combination leads to consistency problems. If you've got a 600-ci engine with nitrous oxide and you're trying to race with a stock suspension and a 9-inch-wide rear slick, you probably don't have a prayer of getting it down the track the same way every time. As long as you aren't overpowering the tires or the suspension, you should be able to make consistent runs.

The key indicator of your car's consistency will be its 60-foot time. If you can get your 60-foot times so that they don't vary more than just a few thousandths of a second from run to run, then you'll have an extremely consistent car to work with, which will help make the task of choosing a dial-in very simple.

Most bracket racers tend to choose a rear slick that is bigger than necessary in order to improve consistency. The combination of a big tire and a loose torque converter can greatly aid consistency.

After you decide on a reasonable engine and transmission combination for your vehicle, it must be accompanied by a suspension that is properly designed, configured, and set up. In turn, the suspension handles the power you're trying to apply to the track. Weight transfer is a critical component of consistent ETs, which is why you'll often see racers adding or removing weight from the rear of their cars and adjusting the front shocks (if equipped) in order to find the perfect balance. A race car that has a lot of power and too much weight on the rear tires might tend to wheelstand excessively, while one that doesn't have enough suspension travel might tend to spin the rear tires.

As with anything else in racing, don't be afraid to play "follow the leader." If you're building a car or just trying to make yours more consistent, find the racers who are successful and see what they're doing. When it comes to suspensions, you don't have to reinvent the wheel, just find a set-up that works for your particular application. Ironically, some people think that, as a general rule, slower cars are more consistent than fast cars. That isn't the case. Pro Stock cars run in the 6.5-second zone at over 210 mph, and they are some of the most consistent race cars in the world. The reason for that is their chassis and suspension were built specifically to accommodate the HP they've got under the hood.

There are other elements involved in building and maintaining a consistent car, including monitoring engine and transmission temperature, and performing a proper burnout, most of which I've already covered. The bottom line here is a race car that is properly constructed and properly driven should be able to make multiple runs on any given day, and all of them should vary no more than a hundredth or two depending on weather and track conditions.

Choosing the Right Dial-In Time

In the first two parts of this chapter I've noted that consistent ETs are generally the by-product of proper driving technique and a well-built race car. If you've been able to introduce both of those elements into your program, then choosing the correct dial-in should be very simple

Many factors affect consistency, but few more than heat. You should make every effort to be sure that your engine and transmission are at the correct temperature before each run. If your engine and transmission are above or below optimal operating temperature, you will find it difficult to stick to your dial-in time.

and straightforward. If you have a car that is extremely consistent and works on just about any racetrack, and your driving skills have advanced to the point where you're able to follow the same routine every time, then you've taken just about all of the guesswork out of the dial-in procedure. It's important to understand that if your driving and car are consistent, then the only variables will be weather and track conditions, and you should already know how to monitor those factors and adjust accordingly.

So, consider a real-world race situation, and see if you can determine what the correct dial-in should be. Imagine for a minute that you've made two time-trial runs on which you and your vehicle have performed flawlessly, and the end result is two very consistent runs of 10.01 and 10.02 seconds. Both of your speeds are virtually identical as well, 135.55 mph on the first run and 136.02 mph on the second. Now, you're about to head into eliminations and it's time to pick your dial-in. What number do you choose? You could just dial a 10.01 seconds, in the hopes that, as long as you and your car remain consistent, you'll be able to repeat your earlier performance. Well, you could take that approach, except there's no guarantee that your next run will be as perfect as your first two. What happens if your car spins the tires ever so slightly? What if the wind shifts and that tailwind becomes a headwind? What if your engine temperature is 160 degrees instead of the usual 170 degrees? These and a host of other variables can affect your performance, and you should always consider these factors when selecting your dial-in. Perhaps a better strategy

There is a number of variables that go into choosing the correct dial-in including weather, track conditions, and the opponent you'll be facing. A successful racer will eliminate as many variables as possible, and in turn, stick to a maintenance, tuning, and preparation routine. That way, the racer can concentrate on coping with the variables out of their control.

Variables, such as wind, will have a much greater affect on your car at the finish line than at the starting line, in the staging lanes, or in the pit area.

might be to dial 10.03 or even 10.04 seconds, so that even if your car's performance slows a bit, you are still in the race. Some experienced racers routinely dial 0.05 to 0.08 second slower than their vehicle will run, just so they know that they'll always be able to run the number. Of course, in order to take that approach you must have supreme confidence in your finish-line driving skills. You must be able to judge your opponent accurately and make each race as close as humanly possible in order for that strategy to be effective.

By "holding" a little ET, that is, dialing a bit slower than your car is capable of running—also known as dialing soft or sandbagging—you will have the ability to win some races even if your opponent has a quicker reaction time than you do. For instance, if your opponent gains a 0.03-second advantage against you on the starting line (0.008- to 0.038-second reaction time) your only real chance to win the race is to pursue him or her all the way to the finish line and then dump him or her by hitting the brakes and/or lifting off the gas. In theory, you should be able to force your opponent into a breakout because you were holding 0.02 to 0.03 second on your dial-in. If you did not hit the brakes, you would probably have broken out yourself. Having that extra little bit "in the bank" allowed you to win a race that you otherwise would have lost. If you had "dialed honest" and chosen a dial-in that matched your car's performance exactly, your opponent would have been in control of the race, and most likely would have been far enough ahead of you at the finish line to be able to hit the brakes and win by a comfortable margin. While all of this might

Accurately reading the track is an important skill for any racer to develop. A close up of the track surface reveals the amount of rubber that has built up in the center of the lane. By closely looking at the texture of the surface, you can determine exactly where the best traction will be found.

In ET-style events that require a dial-in, a portable weather station can be extremely helpful for determining how wind, temperature, humidity, and other factors will affect your car's performance and ET.

Selecting the proper dial-in for each round is one of the many critical decisions that a bracket racer faces during the course of an event. Choose a dial-in that is too quick, and you won't be able to catch your opponent. On the other hand, a dial-in that is too slow may cause you to break out.

sound a bit complicated, it really isn't, especially when you remember that bracket racing is simply an exercise in mathematics. From your opponent's point of view, a package that includes a 0.05-second reaction time and a run that is 0.05 second under the dial-in looks exactly the same as a perfect run.

When selecting a dial-in, it's also important to consider your opponent. If you're paired with a racer who is much faster than you, you'll probably have a difficult time judging him or her at the finish line. You might want to choose an honest dial-in and plan on holding the throttle down all the way to the finish line. Conversely, if you're chasing a really slow car, you'll be faced with some tough decisions near the finish line, so you might also consider an honest dial-in, but in most cases

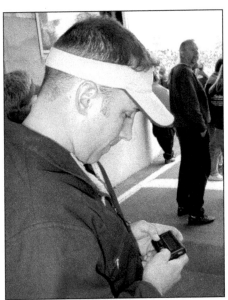

In addition to the portable weather stations, some of the more sophisticated systems also use a pager to relay atmospheric conditions and other pertinent information from the home base (usually a trailer or motor home in the pit area) to the racer.

you'll want to keep a little in the bank just to be safe.

The most important thing to remember about soft dial-in is to adjust your run to hit that exact time. If you've chosen a dial-in that is 0.05 second faster than you think your car can run, you're going to have to scrub off 0.05 second of ET at some point in the run or else you're going to break out. It's that simple.

Some of the tools that will help you when selecting your dial-in are your weather station and your logbook, and you should consult both of them regularly. A review of your previous runs will provide a lot of useful information when it comes time to shoe polish an ET on your windshield. Also, many of the software programs that are currently available have a feature that will help you predict your car's performance; if used properly, they are very accurate.

Starting Line Tactics

To obtain the quickest ET, I recommend shallow staging your car. After your car's wheels have triggered the pre-stage light, slowly inch forward until the wheel breaks the beam for the stage lights. Your vehicle is now shallow staged and the farthest away from the starting line. When the Christmas tree counts down and the car is launched, your car will be given more space to get up to speed before the timing system is triggered. Once your car leaves the line and the timing system starts recording your ET, the car will be carrying more speed off the line, and that speed will be carried all the way to the finish line. As stated many times in this text, consistency is the name of the game in bracket racing. Therefore, you want to stage your car in the same position for each run so you achieve consistent times. If you deep stage on one run and shallow stage the next, it will affect your ET and most likely you will not post consistent runs.

Driving the Finish Line

One thing that most racers can agree on is that driving the finish line, which is the ability to accurately judge the position of your car against that of your opponent as you near the end of the race, is the most difficult element of bracket racing to master. Traveling at speeds of 140 to 170 mph and sometimes faster,

After you've made a few elimination runs, you'll begin to grasp the concept of finish-line driving. Ideally, you'll want to win each race by the smallest margin possible.

Some racers prefer to "dial soft," which means that they choose a dial-in that is a few hundredths slower than their vehicle is capable of running. Dialing soft, or "sandbagging" as it is sometimes called, gives a racer a small margin for error in the event of tire spin or other driver error.

bracket racers often have to make split-second decisions that can dramatically affect the outcome of a race. Which driver is going to cross the finish line first? Do I have enough room to hit the brakes and still finish first? Am I going to break out? What is my opponent going to do? These are just some of the questions that bracket racers must ponder as they head down track during an elimination run. Quite simply, some racers seem to have an innate knack for processing information on the fly and making accurate finish line decisions while others struggle with this element of the game. To make matters worse, unlike the reaction times, there is no practice tree or simulator that will help you master the fine art of finish line driving. The only real way to improve your top-end skills is to make runs, lots of them, and pay close attention each time you are locked in a close side-by-side race. As is often the case, practice does indeed make perfect.

Given the primacy of practice, there are a few things to consider when making your finish-line driving decisions. Obviously, if you and your opponent run about the same speed, then the job of judging his or her vehicle is much easier than racing against someone who is running 20 or 30 mph faster. In most close races, your best course of action is to simply glance over at your opponent's front tire as you approach the finish line, decide who is ahead (and more important who is likely to be ahead at the stripe) and then make your decision accordingly. Remember, the main objective in bracket racing is to make each race as close as possible so if you're well ahead, you'll want to scrub off some speed either by hitting the brakes or lifting

The ability to accurately judge the position of your opponent at or near the finish line and then make a quick decision based on your observation is a skill that all good bracket racers need to have. It usually takes a bit of practice to learn, but it's essential for long-term success.

In many close side-by-side races, you'll often have to make a quick decision to either lift off the throttle or hold it to the floor. It isn't uncommon for two sportsman racers to cross the finish line just a few inches apart.

This shot shows that the competitor in the far lane has placed his front tires about 6 to 8 inches ahead of his opponents as they near the finish line. Barring a breakout, he is likely to get the win.

off the gas, so that you win the race by just a few inches.

In those cases where you've beaten your opponent off the starting line by a large margin, you will most likely be well ahead as you approach the finish line and you can simply ease off the throttle and coast to the victory while he or she tries in vain to catch you. Unfortunately, you won't always have the luxury of being so far ahead and more often than not, you and your opponent will have similar reaction times. As a result, you'll be locked in a close wheel-to-wheel duel all the way to the finish. In those cases, you'll have to do some quick thinking as you race down the track.

In most elimination races, you'll want to start looking for your opponent by the time you reach half track or at the very least by the 1,000-foot mark. If you're driving the faster car, the entire race will be laid out in front of you, and you can quickly decide if your momentum will allow you to pass your slower opponent as you reach the top-end stripe. If you're being chased, it becomes a bit more complicated as you'll either have to turn your head or look in your mirror to find your opponent. Use your rear-view mirror if your car is so equipped. This can be extremely difficult, depending on your opponent's vehicle and the performance differential between the two of you. Imagine that you're driving a 12-second street car, and your opponent is in a 7-second dragster. Now imagine that you're racing at night, and his or her car is painted black. As you head down the track, you scan your mirrors and turn your head to look but can't see a thing. Just as you're about to cross the finish line, you hear the sound of the engine and

As the finish line nears, each driver must be prepared to make a split-second decision whether to hit the brakes or hold the throttle wide open.

At this point, the driver in the far lane has established a clear-cut advantage, so the near lane driver might consider tapping the brake pedal or lifting off the throttle in an effort to win the race via a breakout.

catch a glimpse of his or her car as it zips by. Admittedly, that's an extreme example of the challenges drivers face when it comes to judging an opponent, but it also helps explain why most racers agree that the faster car has the advantage in a bracket race.

There are a few tricks that you can use to help yourself become a better finish-line driver. First off, if you're parked next to your opponent in the staging lanes, take careful note of where his or her front tires are in relation to yours. Position your car so that your front tires are just a few inches in front of your opponent's, and then look over and pick out a spot on the car that indicates that you are positioned correctly. If the other car is longer or shorter than yours, you'll want to keep that in mind as you head down the track. When you hit the finish line, you'll usually want to position your front tires so that they are just a few inches in front of your opponent's, so you should have the same reference view as you did in the staging lanes.

It's also crucial for you to know whether your opponent's front tire, or the nose of his or her car, is going to stop the clocks at the finish line. At many drag strips, the photocells at the finish line are elevated by a few inches, and it's entirely possible that a low-slung front end will stop the clocks a foot or more before the front wheels actually cross the finish line. Many racers have been surprised to lose a race when they knew they were ahead because their opponent stopped the clocks with the front end, so it's important to recognize what your opponent is capable of. Although the NHRA Rulebook mandates that all vehicles have a minimum of 3 inches of ground

In this all-dragster race, note that the driver in the far lane has his head turned to the left as he carefully monitors the progress of his opponent. It's each driver's responsibility to gauge the position of his opponent in relation to the finish line stripe. A racer doesn't want to risk a breakout if a clear-cut lead had been established.

When judging the finish line, you'll want to check your opponent's position on the track in relation to your own as quickly as possible. In most cases, you'll have just a split second in order to decide whether to take the stripe or lift off the gas and let your opponent cross the finish line first, risking a breakout.

clearance that clearance is measured when the car is standing still. Under hard deceleration, a front end will tend to "dip," especially if the shocks and springs use a "soft" setting. If your opponent hits the brakes near the finish line, his or her front end might drop far enough to stop the timers even if it was well above the 3-inch minimum.

In a close side-by-side race, your opponent is likely to be just as conscious of your position on the track as you are of his or hers. Your opponent will also be looking at you and making the same critical decisions as you are. That's why it's important that you be able to react quickly and make split-second adjustments to your strategy. If, for instance, you are ahead and you see your opponent's front end dip, that's a clear indication of pushing hard on the brakes. Most likely, he or she's realized that you can't be caught and has decided to "cut you loose" in the hopes that you will break out. In this case, your

best course of action is to tap the brake pedal yourself in an effort to avoid a breakout. As long as your dial-in is accurate, you're probably close to your dial-in time and should win the race.

Against astute opponents, you'll also want to try to make your decision as late as possible, so they won't have time to respond. If you decide to hit the brakes and send them on their way, and you start slowing at the 1,100-foot mark, then they will have plenty of time, the last 220 feet of the racetrack, to counter your move. Ideally, you want to handcuff them so that when you decide to hit the brakes, they won't have enough time or enough distance to hit the brakes alongside of you.

There are essentially just four different scenarios that you'll face when driving the top end:

1. You are ahead of your opponent and your momentum will keep you ahead.

2. You are ahead and your opponent is going to pass you before the finish line.
3. Your opponent is ahead and, with his or her momentum, will stay ahead.
4. Your opponent is ahead and you are going to pass him or her before the finish line.

In time, you will learn to identify each of these scenarios and will develop the ability to act accordingly, making the necessary adjustments in order to maximize your odds of winning the race. Learning to judge the finish line isn't easy, but it is something that you're going to have to learn in order to have long-term success in bracket racing. In this day and age, almost every bracket racer is capable of hitting the Christmas tree on a consistent basis, and with all of the modern technology available, race cars are more consistent than ever, so the only real edge a driver has comes by driving the finish line well.

In this race, the driver in the far lane has moved his vehicle to the far left of the racing groove in an effort to get a better view as he closes in on his opponent. This will allow him to more accurately judge the distance between the two vehicles.

THE PSYCHOLOGY OF DRAG RACING

Noted Hall of Fame baseball catcher Yogi Berra once noted, "Baseball is 90 percent mental; the other half is physical." While Yogi's math skills may have been a bit fuzzy, it could easily be argued that his philosophy also applies to drag racing. At the risk of oversimplifying the matter, drag racing, particularly in the case of ET bracket racing, is nothing more than a highly evolved cerebral exercise that happens to be played out using high-performance vehicles. While it's true that any successful racer must have the right equipment, and it is also true that having a fast car can help make up for a lot of mental or driving errors, the simple fact is that you will usually succeed in drag racing by out-thinking and out-witting your opponents rather than out-muscling them.

Some people have the mistaken belief that it takes a tremendous amount of physical strength to drive

The ability to focus, react quickly, and stay calm under pressure are all common traits that most successful drag racers possess. Your beliefs, attitude, and approach will greatly affect the outcome of each race. A successful racer will always critically examine his or her own performance and look for ways to improve.

One common trait that most successful drag racers share is the ability to think and react quickly and make split-second decisions when necessary.

a race car, but that's generally not the case. While physical strength may be necessary in certain situations to maintain proper car control, it is just a very small part of the many components that make up a successful race car driver. Perhaps some people have confused strength with agility, which is certainly a quality trait for a race car driver. In most cases, though, driving a properly set up race car should require minimal physical exertion. As we've noted earlier, drag racing is so popular because all people can enjoy the sport, regardless of strength, size, age, race, or gender.

One common trait that most good racers share is the ability to think and react quickly. The ability to process information quickly is essential, especially as a driver begins to advance into some of drag racing's quicker classes. Some of the best drag racers seem to be blessed with natural ability and seem to instinctively know exactly what to do and when to do it. Others need constant practice in order to refine their skills. No matter which of these groups you fall into, it's important to understand that the best way to become a consistent winner is to continually think and re-think each of the decisions you face regarding your racing operation. Like any other athlete, a racer becomes successful by combining dedication, skill, and hard work.

Sizing Up the Competition

Many of the self-help books that have been previously written on drag racing preach that you should treat every opponent equally and concentrate on doing the same thing each and every time you make a run. Frankly, that might be the worst piece of advice that you can hear. Why would you want to treat every opponent the same when it's obvious that all racers are different, and each one is likely to have a unique combination of traits, which sets them apart from their peers? NFL coaches don't use the same game plan for each of their opponents and neither should you.

When sizing up your competition, some things should be fairly obvious. For instance, if your opponent has "12-time track champion" lettered boldly on the sides of his or her race car, then it should be fairly obvious that he or she is someone with a lot of experience. You have every reason to believe that you are facing a good racer, and that it is probably going to take a very good run in order to win. Conversely, if your opponent is a novice, it's relatively easy to spot because of some of the common rookie mistakes, such as struggling to perform a proper burnout or having difficulty understanding how the staging system and Christmas tree function. If you're paired with an obvious beginner, naturally, you should adjust your strategy accordingly. Nothing feels worse than red-lighting by a few thousandths of a second while your inexperienced opponent wins after fumbling around on the starting line, leaving long after the green light is on and then compounding the error by running way off his or her dial-in.

If you plan to race at the same track week after week, it won't take long for you to spot specific tendencies in your opponents and you should take note of them and use them to your advantage whenever possible. Is there a racer at your track who absolutely refuses to stage first? Then you might consider countering this stubbornness by rushing in and staging quickly, so that he or she'll be the one feeling the pressure instead of you.

As if often the case in sports, it helps to know each of your opponents, and their tendencies. Once you learn how your opponent races, you can usually identify a weakness and formulate a game plan to beat them. However, most racers will be sizing you up and looking to exploit your weaknesses as well.

What about the racer who always "sandbags" and chooses a dial-in that is five or six hundredths slower than his or her car is capable of running? If you're involved in a close race, you're probably going to want to hit the brakes or lift off the gas near the finish line and let him or her cross the stripe first as a prime candidate for a breakout. There are some drivers who hold an "old school" mentality; if they are capable of crossing the finish line first, they'll do it every time.

In another example, maybe you've noticed that there is one poor competitor at your local track who routinely wins the first two or three rounds every Saturday afternoon, and then has trouble adjusting when the sun begins to set and frequently red-lights when it gets dark. Don't you think it would be a good idea to make sure you don't red-light against this person?

These are just some of the small but very important bits of informa-tion that you should take note of and file away for future reference. Once again, it's to your benefit to take plenty of notes and learn how to use them effectively.

As you improve your racing skills and you hopefully begin to move into faster and more competitive classes, you're bound to notice that the difference between skill levels among competitors isn't as pro-nounced as it once was. For compar-ison's sake, as a beginning golfer, it is possible for you to trim 20 or more strokes off your game as you con-tinue to practice, learn, and improve. However, it is impossible for the world's top golfers on the PGA tour to improve by 20 strokes or even 10 strokes. In drag racing's most com-petitive classes, you're likely to find that almost every driver is capable of achieving competitive reaction times on just about every run. More often than not, they're going to drive their race car, whether it's a Top Fuel drag-ster or an ET bracket car, in a manner that gives them the best chance to win. Earlier in this chapter, you learned about adjusting your game plan to suit each opponent, but once you find yourself competing in the same arena as a lot of talented and experienced racers, the difference in skill level between you and your opponents should be so minimal that you probably shouldn't deviate much from your established routine. In this instance, it would probably be a mistake to back off on your reac-tion times unless it's very obvious that your opponent is struggling. As is the case with our amateur golfer, as you improve you'll reach a point of diminishing returns in regards to skill level between you and your competitors.

If you race at the same track every week, it won't take long for you to learn who your opponents are and how they race. After you've familiarized yourself with your competition, you can begin to make adjustments to your own strategy.

You can pick up a lot of information on your opponents and their race cars just by walking through the staging lanes. You should also take note of their on-track performance. You should spend the time to observe competitors' runs in your class. If you're observant, you will likely recognize each driver's distinctive approach to racing and their unique style.

Visualization for Racing

In the early 1980s, Frank Hawley won a pair of NHRA Funny Car championships behind the wheel of the famed Chi-Town Hustler. Hawley later drove Darrell Gwynn's Top Fuel dragster and was one of just a handful of individuals who have won NHRA events in both Top Fuel and Funny Car. However, Hawley's greatest contribution to drag racing isn't his many race wins or championships, but rather his work in establishing the first official Drag Racing School in Gainesville, Florida. For more than 20 years, Hawley has taught thousands of students how to drag race and he's helped launch the careers of many championship-winning drivers.

Hawley has also performed some of the most extensive research ever done on the mental aspects of drag racing, and his studies have yielded some great advice for both beginners and experienced racers alike. One of the many lessons that Hawley teaches to his students is the importance of mental visualization, also known as mental rehearsal, which involves using your imagination to simulate the exact details of a perfect run. Widely used as part of sports psychology, mental visualization can be extremely helpful to drag racers because it isn't always possible to make run after run down a drag strip in order to improve your skills.

In order to effectively use mental visualization, you must first be good at pretending. It doesn't matter if you're strapped into your race car in the shop or sitting at home on the couch, you should be able to, from memory, recall everything you see, hear, touch, and feel when you're making a run. Over and over and over again, you should imagine each run in minute detail, until each action becomes virtually automatic. The benefits of visualization not only include making perfect runs, but also prepare you for when things don't go exactly as planned. Imagining yourself activating a fire extinguisher or finding the parachute release lever in an emergency situation can be extremely helpful when and if the real thing occurs. The reason that mental visualization works is that part of your mind doesn't know the difference between actually driving or just imagining that you're driving.

In addition to mental visualization, you should also establish a detailed procedure for each run. Everything you do before and during a run should be written down in great detail and committed to memory. You should attempt to follow your notes to the letter until each individual movement becomes

Any time you make a run, it's important to do so with a clear head. The race track is a hive of constant activity and distraction. When you're in the car you need to effectively shut all of that out and transition into a zone of deep concentration. This way, you will be focused on properly executing the entire sequence of actions required to put together a successful run.

As you begin to progress to faster classes and more advanced race cars, you're likely to find that the overall difference in skill level between drivers doesn't vary much. Here, the small differences are amplified and as a consequence the margin between victory and defeat can be very minute.

automatic, and you can perform them without thought or hesitation. Once you've mastered the elements of mental visualization, you should have corrected most if not all of your bad habits and uncluttered your mind so that you can fully concentrate on driving your car to the best of your ability.

Avoiding Distractions

Would it surprise you to know that some of drag racing's best drivers

Many successful racers hone their driving skills using a technique called mental visualization, which uses imagination and mental imagery to simulate the exact details of a run. By going through a run in your head, you can program yourself to perform at your best by taking all the necessary actions. In addition, you can anticipate the actions of your competitors and how to respond to them.

aren't capable of changing a spark plug? While that might be oversimplifying the matter a bit, it's not far from the truth. Some drivers are hired simply for driving. However, it's also true that there are plenty of great racers who are also great mechanics, tuners, engine builders, and crew chiefs. Hired drivers don't worry about the mechanical aspects of their racing operation because they don't have to. But how can these drivers succeed if they don't know how the car works? The short answer is that some drivers who are not mechanically inclined are able to succeed simply because they are able to devote their full and undivided attention to driving the race car. While these drivers are strapped into their race cars, they're able to completely focus on the task at hand. They're not concerned about the tune-up, or the clutch and chassis settings, and as a result they've eliminated the source of many potential distractions.

Obviously, most bracket and sportsman class racers don't have the luxury of hiring a full-time crew so that they can concentrate solely on driving. However, it doesn't mean that they can't learn how to become better racers by minimizing outside distractions. If you're like most amateur or sportsman racers, you make all the tuning calls on your race car and you are the driver, but it's important that you be able to differentiate between the two roles. As a driver, once you fasten your helmet and fire the engine, you need to understand that you've made the transition from mechanic to driver and driving is your top priority. You can no longer agonize over the adjustments you made before the run. Unless you have the ability to make adjustments on the fly, such as changing a delay box or throttle-stop setting or adjusting the starting-line RPM, the setup you left the pits with is the one that will be with you as you go down the

Many race car drivers practice mental visualization, which involves replaying each run over and over in your mind until all of your movements become routine. Even if you don't visualize your run, spending a few minutes in solitude prior to each run can greatly help your concentration.

track. It does no good to distract yourself by worrying about factors that are now out of your control.

One lesson that has been repeated several times in this book is the importance of having a clear head any time you make a run. The ability to ignore potential distractions is essential throughout the entire duration of your run, from burnout box to shutdown area, and it's particularly critical when you're in the stage beams, preparing to react to the Christmas tree. At that point, even a minor distraction, one that affects your concentration by a couple of hundredths of a second or even a few thousandths, can often spell the difference between winning and losing.

Honesty Is the Best Policy

One of the best traits that any racer can posses is the ability to recognize mistakes and learn from them so that they aren't repeated. Of course, in order to learn from a mistake, a racer must first be able to admit that he or she has actually

made one, which is understandably difficult for some racers to do. If you're struggling to win races, mired in an extended slump, or if you just simply want to become a better race-car driver, you won't fix your problems by blaming your car, your crew, your engine builder, or anyone else. Don't let your ego get the best of you. If one of your crewmembers or a fellow racer tells you that you're not driving your car properly, don't get mad and certainly don't ignore their advice. Take it to heart and learn from it.

There are some racers who simply can't or won't claim responsibility for losing a race. They seem to have an excuse for every loss and none of them involve poor driving or a lack of focus on their part. They find it nearly impossible to acknowledge that their opponent simply did a better job than they did. The point here is that if you try hard enough, you can come up with an excuse, no matter how lame or untrue, to cover just about any loss. If that doesn't work, you can always just claim that your opponent is an inferior driver

who was simply lucky to beat you. However, you should be able to acknowledge that excuses won't help make you a better racer.

To put it another way, if you lost a race, there is a reason why you lost and it's your job to find it, no matter how painful that may be. Maybe it wasn't your fault but maybe it was. Did your car spin the tires because the track was slick or did you cause them to spin with a poorly executed burnout? Was your reaction time late because the engine was cold and stumbled or did you simply lose your concentration? If you're willing to make an honest evaluation of the situation, you're likely to find that your results will improve in short order. It's also important to continually analyze your wins and your losses because you can lean just as much by the things you did correctly as you can by recognizing your mistakes.

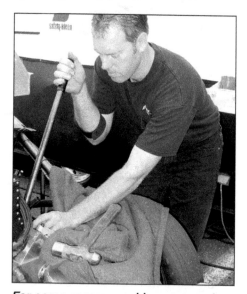

For some racers, working on cars is an enjoyable way to pass the time between runs and a welcome diversion from the pressures of driving. Others do their best when they can focus solely on driving. Which category do you fall into?

Oftentimes, an opponent in the other lane or fans in the stands can be a distraction. When you're staged and preparing to race, you've got to block them out and concentrate on the Christmas tree. For each run, you have one opportunity to launch and drive the top end of the track.

A smart racer is one who does not make excuses, but rather learns from his or her mistakes and takes steps to make sure they aren't repeated. Racing, of course, is a learning process. All professional drivers have made their fair share of mistakes as they advanced through the ranks.

Tricks of the Trade

Most of the racers you'll encounter anywhere in the country are friendly and honest people who share the same passion for racing and high-performance vehicles as you do. However, it is important to fully understand that drag racing is an extremely competitive sport and many racers are willing to do whatever it takes, within the rules, to give themselves an advantage over a competitor. Some racers have no problem playing mind games with their opponents if they feel that it will benefit them and some of the tricks in their arsenals include trash talk, lane swaps, starting line burn-downs, and just about anything else they believe will confuse, intimidate, or otherwise distract an opponent.

Most of the gamesmanship that goes on at races occurs in the staging lanes, just as competitors are paired and preparing to race. Most often, competitors who are about to race will simply wish each other a safe race and return to their vehicles. For some, however, a face-to-face meeting with an opponent presents an opportunity to gain the upper hand. In some cases, a driver who has earned lane choice will simply exercise his or her advantage and many opponents will race a lane that they are unfamiliar with. In other words, if you've won four straight races in the left lane and you don't have lane choice for the following round, there is a good chance that your opponent will force you to move to the right lane, even after making most of his or her runs in the right lane. This is simply doing whatever can be done in order to break your rhythm.

To cite another example, your opponent might approach you and show you time slips from previous rounds, especially if his or her reaction times have been very competitive. This is an effort to intimidate you by showing you how good he or she is. This might be combined with a bit of trash talking, reciting the statistics of his or her impressive résumé, while pointing out perceived flaws in your program. In most cases, a little trash talking is harmless as long as your opponent doesn't cross the line by using obscene or threatening language. However, be aware that unsportsmanlike conduct can result in fines, loss of points, and other consequences. Rather than engage in a war of words, your best response is usually to get in your car and then do the best job you can as a driver. More often than not, you'll be the one who has the last laugh.

The burn-down has been around since the dawn of the Christmas-tree starting system. To some drivers, it's also an effective tool that they

While most racers are very friendly and helpful, it is common for some to attempt to intimidate or distract their opponents with a bit of pre-race trash talking. These mind games often occur in the staging lanes. Recognize trash talking for what it is, and don't let it interfere with your game plan.

believe helps them win races. It's a simple fact that some drivers don't like to stage before their opponent stages and when two drivers share that mentality, the stage is set for a burn-down. During a burn-down, both drivers sit in the pre-stage beams, with neither driver willing to make the first move into the fully staged position.

In professional classes, such as Pro Stock, it's common for a burn-down to last a minute or more while the fans in the stands go wild, but if you're bracket racing at your local track, the official starter likely will intervene after 30 seconds or so. When you engage in a burn-down, you're holding up the entire program and you're walking a fine line since failure to obey a starter's directions could be grounds for disqualification or other penalties. Also, your engine might get too hot and your tires might get too cold, drastically affecting the performance of your car. You might prove your point by forcing your stubborn opponent to stage first, but it might ultimately cost you the race if your car is not up to snuff.

How you treat your fellow racers is entirely up to you. Some racers are of the opinion that drag racing isn't a popularity contest, and if trash talking and other forms of trickery will help them win races, they're willing to engage in these tactics. Others value the camaraderie that often goes with racing and go to great lengths to avoid confrontations. If you choose the former, you should do so with the understanding that it probably won't take long for you to develop a reputation, and your fellow drivers will probably quickly learn to either ignore or combat your trash talk. The choice is up to you.

Occasionally, a pair of racers is each determined to make their opponent stage first. When that happens, a burn down often follows. Some burn downs can last a minute or more, but among sportsman racers, it's rarely more than just a few seconds.

Rather than engage in mental warfare, most racers simply prefer to strap themselves into their cars and go racing.

Having a mechanically sound race car can go a long way towards improving a racer's state of mind, which is why it's important to establish and keep a regular maintenance routine. A last-minute check in staging is a good way to confirm the car is ready to run.

RACER MATH

From ETs to HP ratings, reaction times, and true-win margins, the entire sport of drag racing seems to be overflowing with numbers. It can all seem a bit confusing, even to an experienced racer. What are these numbers? What do they all mean? And, more importantly, how can I use them to my advantage?

Among the many skills that any good racer should possess is a basic understanding of mathematics and how it relates to drag racing. If that sentence scares you, don't worry; we're not talking about doctorate-level quantum physics or even college algebra, but rather just some elementary arithmetic calculations

that are often nothing more than simple addition, subtraction, multiplication, and division. For all racing intents and purposes, if you can pass a fifth-grade math test then you're capable of performing all the computations necessary to become a successful racer. Like most other endeavors, you just have to be willing to put forth a little time and effort.

How to Determine True-Win Margin

If you've raced for any length of time you've no doubt been involved in some close side-by-side races. In fact, oftentimes the outcome of a race is too close to call with the naked eye, which is why track operators invest many thousands of dollars in state-of-the-art timing equipment that can determine the winner of each race with incredible accuracy. Your time slip will tell you how close each race was, but that figure is expressed in ET, not distance. Your time slip may tell you that you won or lost a race by 0.01 sec, but do you really know how close that is?

From reaction times to ETs, numbers play a significant role in drag racing, which makes it necessary for all racers to have an understanding of basic mathematics.

Were you ahead at the finish line by 3 inches or 2 feet?

In order to convert the true-win margin from time to distance, take the margin of victory as listed on the time slip (MOV), multiply it by the speed of the first vehicle to reach the finish line, and then multiply that sum by 1.47525. This will give you the margin of victory expressed in feet or inches (if the number is less than 1, simply multiply by 12 in order to determine inches). It is also important to note that because speed is not determined precisely at the finish line, but rather calculated using a 66-foot speed trap, there is a margin of error of about plus-or-minus 1 percent.

You should make a habit of using this formula to determine how close each of your side-by-side races was and you should catalog your results, no matter if you won or lost. Your result will help to determine how accurately you're judging your opponents at the finish line. This is obviously a critical element of bracket racing because your objective is to win each race by the smallest margin possible. If you're like most racers you will probably find that some races, while they appeared close from the driver's seat, were actually not as tight as you first believed them to be. There is simple explanation for this. Traveling at high speeds, your brain is attempting to process a lot of information in a very short amount of time and small details, such as the position of your opponent's front tires, can often be overlooked or misjudged. Once you've made a lot of runs in competition, you should find that your finish-line skills are improved, but it's still a great idea to log the margin of victory in all of your races.

Tracking margin of victory can also help you learn a lot about how your opponents race. If you race

Using a simple math formula that converts ET into distance, you can determine exactly how close each race was at the finish line. To calculate true-win margin from time to distance, use the margin of victory (MOV) on the time slip, multiply it by the speed of the first vehicle to reach the finish line, and then multiply that sum by 1.47525. The margin of victory will be expressed in feet or inches (if the number is less than 1, simply multiply by 12 in order to determine inches).

The ET and speed that appears on the scoreboard after each run are just a few of the numbers that define drag racing. After you've completed your run, you will receive a timing slip with the same information from the timing shack.

A simple sliding power/speed calculator can be useful when trying to determine how fast your vehicle should run or how much HP your engine has.

It's vital to keep detailed records of your car's performance. At the very least, you should keep a logbook and record the data from every run you make down the drag strip. It's also a good idea to keep a log book of the driver's performance. It's gives you the chance to review your performance and make plans for improving.

Cataloging the numbers from your previous runs can help you accurately predict your vehicle's performance on future runs. A good idea is to catalog all your runs in a Microsoft Excel-type spreadsheet program, so you can evaluate and analyze the data to improve your performance and consistency.

against the same opponent several times and are consistently beaten by a small margin of victory, then he or she is obviously a skilled racer and you might have to consider adjusting your strategy the next time you meet on the track. As a general rule, you can't control what your opponent does so it's imperative that you take care of business in your own lane. However, if you're consistently being out-driven, then maybe you need to make an adjustment to better your reaction times, or to rethink your dial-in strategy.

Using Math to Help Predict Performance

If you regularly compete at an eighth-mile drag strip and want to know what your car will run on a quarter-mile track, you can simply multiply your eighth-mile ET by 1.55 in order to get a quarter-mile time that is reasonably accurate. Likewise, you can multiply your eighth-mile speed by 1.25 in order to get a good idea of what your vehicle's top speed would be on a quarter-mile run. The same formulas can also be used to convert a 330-foot clocking to eighth-mile numbers.

If you're bracket racing during eliminations and have to lift off the gas or hit the brakes before the finish line in order to avoid a breakout, you can use your incremental numbers to determine what your car would have run if you had held the throttle down to the finish line. This can be accomplished by reviewing the data from your last full-throttle run, usually on a time trial, and finding the 1,000-foot-to-1,320-foot time. As long as you were under power to the 1,000-foot mark on your elimination run, you can simply add your

1,000-foot-to-1,320-foot time from the previous run to get an idea of what you would have run since this number rarely varies by more than a few thousandths of a second.

In those rare cases when you lifted before the 1,000-foot mark, you can use your back-half numbers (660 feet to 1,320 feet) from a previous run in order to make the same calculation. This method isn't quite as accurate as the 1,000-foot-to-1,320-foot method, but it's pretty close and can be very helpful when choosing a dial-in during elimination rounds.

Once you've logged a large number of runs in your database (see below) you'll instinctively know how much ET you've "killed" or lost just about any time you hit the brakes or take your foot off the gas before the finish line. In a close race, you'll know how much time you won or lost by, what your vehicle was going to run, and more often than not, that information will be extremely helpful to you in subsequent rounds.

Tracking Your Round-Win Average

Much like baseball players monitoring batting averages or golfers averaging scores in order to determine a proper handicap, tracking your round-win average over the course of a full season, or from year to year, can be a great way to track your progress as you gain experience and confidence.

Your round-win average can be determined simply by dividing your round wins by the number of elimination rounds you've participated in. For example, if you've raced in 24 elimination rounds and won 11 of them, your average would be .458 (11 / 24 = .458333).

By properly interpreting and evaluating the data provided by previous runs, you can usually come up with an accurate prediction of how your vehicle will perform on future runs. The more you understand the factors that produced a particular result, the more you will be better able to adjust the car and your driving technique.

Using a laptop computer, you can create a spreadsheet that stores volumes of data including your elapsed times, reaction times, round-win average, and similar information regarding your opponents.

After establishing a record-keeping routine, you'll go into every race armed with the necessary information. In order to run competitively, you need to make the most of the information you gather. You can be sure that your competitors are evaluating and analyzing the data and looking for a way to run faster and more consistently.

One of the easiest things drivers can to do improve results is to pay attention to their entire racing environment, including air and track conditions, their opponents, and their own race car.

Many racers choose to use video cameras to record their runs. A post-race review of the video can reveal much about the vehicle, the driver, and the condition of the race track. A high-resolution picture and the ability to review the footage frame by frame allows you to carefully review each aspect of the run, acquire new information, and formulate the appropriate game plan.

Once you've established your round-win average, you'll quickly realize that it's a great motivator, as you'll continually strive to improve your results. If your average is above 50 percent, that means that you are a better-than-average racer and the odds are in your favor every time you stage. Of course, like most averages, the more rounds you run, the more accurate your average will be. Much like a baseball player who goes five-for-five on opening day, winning your first event of the season will give you a perfect 1.000 average but it's obviously not possible to maintain that average for an entire season. Still, it is not unheard of for some of the best sportsman racers in the country to post win percentages above 70 percent, though realistically anything above the 55 to 60-percent range is considered excellent.

Recording Your Runs

The following list includes 50 bits of important data that should be recorded every time you make a run down a drag strip. At first glance, logging all 50 items might seem to be overkill, and in some instances a particular category won't apply to your vehicle or the type of racing. However, used properly, an accurate database can be a valued resource in your ongoing quest to become a more successful racer.

While it's possible to preserve racing data in a logbook or even a simple notebook, a better idea is to use a computer-generated spreadsheet, which allows for greater sorting capabilities, giving you the opportunity to quickly and easily spot trends and patterns.

Most of the information included in your data sheet can be quickly copied from a time slip while other categories will require some note-taking and simple arithmetic. Remember, your database will grow with each passing race and it will become more and more useful as a tuning tool. For example, if you red-light just once every 20 runs over a four-year period and all of a sudden start red-lighting once every 10 runs, you'll quickly be able to identify the problem. You can take the proper steps to correct it rather than just thinking to yourself, "Gee, I seem to be red-lighting more than I used to." The bottom line is that using a spreadsheet will help eliminate a lot of the guesswork from your racing operation.

Here are some of the topics you should consider including in your database:

1. Name and characteristics of the track

The name is pretty basic information, but important especially if you race at more than one track since each racetrack is likely to have very different characteristics especially in regards to traction, rollout, and weather conditions. From your track inspections, you should note other important characteristics, suchas as length of shutdown area, the location of the turnouts, where the safety crews are positions, and how the top end is configured in the event you have difficulty stopping.

2. Track distance (quarter-mile, eighth-mile, or other as measured)

Interestingly, although quarter-mile (1,320 feet) and eighth-mile (660-feet) are standardized distances, some tracks are actually longer or shorter. In addition, some tracks have a tendency to run up or down hill, significantly affecting performance.

3. Day of the week

Why should this matter? Well, if your results are noticeably better on Sunday afternoons than on Friday nights, it could be because you've worked all week and are tired when you get to the races. Or perhaps you've partied on Saturday night and have a tendency to struggle during races held Sunday afternoon. The ability to sort days will allow you to spot emerging trends that might help or hurt your win percentage and address personal habits that might affect your performance.

4. Vehicle

If you race more than one car, truck, or motorcycle, it's important to note this.

5. Time of day

Every racer is affected by the change in lighting from day to night, so it's important to know when you've made your runs. Also, many tracks have vastly different characteristics from day to night, such as fog in the morning and dew in the late evening, so you'll be able to track that here. In this space you can also take note of minute details such as daylight savings time.

6. Run status (timed trial, qualifying, or eliminations)

This can be used to quickly sort results on a spreadsheet using some common abbreviations such as TT1 for time trial 1 or E2 for round 2 of eliminations.

Although the ultimate goal is consistency, most racers have a tendency to drive very differently in eliminations, particularly in the late rounds, and this data will again help you spot personal trends and make necessary adjustments.

7. Ambient air temperature

For this, you'll need a weather station in your pit, or at the very least, a good thermometer. Remember that temperature can change quickly and the temperature on the racetrack might be different from what it is in your pit area.

8. Barometric pressure

Again, this data should come from a weather station since changes in barometric pressure can have a big impact on performance. As a side note, if you're going to use a weather station, try to use the same one at all times because chances are no two will provide the exact same reading.

9. Relative humidity

This is another weather variation that can affect your vehicle's performance. Note that items 7 through 9 on this list can be accompanied by a reading of corrected elevation in feet but should also be logged independently in order to more accurately monitor the affect that atmospheric conditions have on your vehicle.

10. Wind speed

Wind speed should be recorded in MPH using a gauge. Remember that the wind speed in the pit area or staging lanes is often very different from the wind speed on the racetrack. In fact, it's usually best to get a wind-speed reading at or near the finish line since this will have the greatest impact on your vehicle's performance.

11. Wind direction

Knowing how hard the wind is blowing is one thing, but it's also important to know which direction it is blowing. It's also difficult to just enter north, south, east, or west since, obviously, not all tracks face the same direction. Use specific symbols, of your choosing, so that you'll know whether you were facing a headwind, tailwind, or a crosswind.

12. Engine water temperature

It pays to invest in a quality water-temperature gauge, especially one with a digital readout, since just 2 or 3 degrees of engine temperature can affect performance, especially in street-legal cars.

13. Oil pressure

Part of your pre-race routine should include checking your oil pressure just before you pull into the staging beams because a decrease in oil pressure is usually a sign of a serious mechanical problem. Logging this information should be part of your regular maintenance routine.

14. Engine RPM at launch

This is pretty much self explanatory, especially since many sportsman/bracket racers adjust starting-line RPM to adjust their reaction times. If you're using a two-step ignition you'll know your starting-line RPM in advance. A tachometer with recording/playback capabilities can also be useful here. Once you've built up your database, you'll be able to tell exactly how much an increase/decrease in RPM affects your car's performance and your reaction time.

15. Left lane or right lane

At many tracks, there is a significant difference in rollout, traction, and lighting conditions from lane to lane so it's important to note where you've made your runs. Again, with enough data, you'll be able to know exactly how much of a difference.

16. Staged status

Were you shallow staged or did you roll in so deep that you nearly turned off the pre-stage light? Make a notation here and you won't have to wonder why you suddenly red-lighted or why your car suddenly slowed. If you want, you can assign a numerical value to your stage position. For example, "1" for very shallow, "2" for normal, and "3" for deep staged. With this info, you'll be able to fine tune your reaction times. For instance, if all of your No. 3 lights are red, then you know that you've staged too deeply on those runs.

17. Front/rear tire pressure

For accuracy's sake, this should be one of the last things you do before making each run. It's best to have a crewmember adjust and record tire pressure just before you pull out on to the race track. Remember, front tire pressure affects reaction time so it should always be included in your data.

18. Reaction time prediction

Before each run, you should predict what your reaction time will be. Why? Because you should always have a game plan. If you've set up your car to have a 0.015-second reaction time and you miss your target, you should be able to quickly determine whether you or your car is at fault. You should use every run as a way to learn how to set up your car to hit a specific target.

19. Reaction time

Keeping a running total of your reaction times will not only allow you to make adjustments during each race, but it will also allow you to keep a season-long or even a career average. Obviously, you

should also compare your results with your pre-race prediction.

20. Delay-box settings

If you use a delay box, you'll want to record your settings on each run. This data will also help you make necessary adjustments from track to track and from day to night racing.

21. Throttle stop settings

This applies almost exclusively to Super-class racers who are using a timed throttle stop in order to hit a target index. All throttle-stop settings should be monitored and logged from each run.

22. 60-foot ET

Printed on virtually all time slips, your 60-foot clocking is one of the most important numbers you'll get from each run. Comparing 60-foot numbers from run to run will help you know if your car is spinning the tires.

23. 60-foot-to-330-foot ET

This number isn't on your time slip but can be determined via simple subtraction—subtract 60 from 330. This is beyond the area where most race cars will spin the tires, so this number can be used to tell if your car has a stumble or bog. It can also be useful to determine how well you've hit your shift points, especially in a manually shifted car.

24. 330-foot ET

This is noted on the time slip. Again, this number can be an indicator of your car's performance early in the run. For example, if your car begins to slow in 330 feet, it could be an indicator of a faulty torque converter or something similar.

25. 330-foot-to-660-foot ET

Another number that can be obtained by using simple subtraction, logging this number can be especially beneficial to Super-class racers who use throttle stops.

26. 660-foot ET prediction

You should predict your eighth-mile and quarter-mile ETs on all runs, even during time trials. Analyzing this data will help you learn to dial your car. This can be especially useful if you regularly switch between quarter- and eighth-mile tracks.

27. 660-foot ET

This is noted on your time slip. An indicator of your car's performance at half-track, it should also be compared with your prediction.

28. 660-foot speed

This number should be printed on most time slips. By the time you reach half-track, your car will begin to be affected by winds so keeping track of your speeds will allow you to make any necessary adjustments to your dial-in.

29. Back-half

This is your quarter-mile ET minus your eighth-mile. For bracket racers who lift off the throttle or hit the brakes before the finish line, it can be used to determine what your car would have run on a full-throttle pass. This information is an essential component in determining dial-ins. Comparing back-half numbers will also help to determine the effects that wind and other weather-related conditions have on your car.

30. 660-foot to 1,000-foot ET

More incremental numbers that can help you fine-tune your car and determine a proper dial-in.

31. 1,000-foot ET

Information that should be readily available on most time slips. During bracket-racing eliminations, you'll almost always be under full power to the 1,000-foot mark so this number should be relatively consistent from run to run.

32. 1,000-foot to 1,320-foot ET

This is the last incremental number you'll encounter in quarter-mile racing and as such, it seldom varies by more than a few thousandths of a second. Again, logging this data can be useful in all forms of sportsman racing.

33. 1,320-foot ET prediction

Using the data in your logbook, your weather station readings, and the results of previous runs, you should be able to predict your ET on every run with a reasonable amount of accuracy. If your car suddenly runs slower than you expect, it could be an indicator of a mechanical problem. Conversely, a car that runs much quicker than expected could be benefiting from a drastic change in weather.

34. Dial-in

This should always be compared to your dial-in prediction in order to determine how well you know your vehicle and its tendencies.

35. 1,320-foot ET

Your quarter-mile ET, measured to the thousandth of a second, is perhaps the most popular number in drag racing.

36. 1,320-foot speed

Measured in MPH, this number is indicated by a set of timers placed 66 feet before the finish line and the actual finish-line clocks. It is actually an average of your top speed in the last 66 feet of the track rather than a true finish-line speed. Bracket racers who hit the brakes during eliminations to avoid a breakout will often notice a drastic difference in top speed from run to run.

37. ET package

This number is determined by adding your ET relative to your dial-in and your reaction time. For example, a driver who had a 0.021 reaction time and ran a 9.927 on his or her 9.91 dial would calculate a package of 0.038 seconds. This data, which can be calculated automatically using a Microsoft Excel-type spreadsheet file, will help you determine how close each race is.

38. Package prediction

In keeping with our theme of always going to the starting line with a game plan, you should predict what your package will be in advance. For instance, if you are set up for a 0.010 reaction time and you believe your car is dialed to run within 1/100 of its performance potential, then you are aiming for a 0.020 package. A constant analysis of this data will help you become a better finish-line driver.

39. Braking point

This information is for bracket racers only and is really just an educated guess. On many side-by-side elimination runs, you'll either be off the gas or hitting the brakes before the finish line. It's helpful to know exactly where you lifted, so look for landmarks on the track, timing markers, guardrail signs, light poles, etc., and try to identify and record them for future reference.

40. Wins

In the end, this is the most important statistic on your data sheet. Keeping a running total of your wins will help you monitor your progress or identify a slump.

41. Losses

The same as above, tracking losses will help you identify trends and focus your energies on fixing mental and/or mechanical errors.

42. Bye runs

Racers tend to drive much differently when there is no opponent in the opposite lane, so it's important to be able to separate your bye runs from other run data. A bye run during eliminations often represents your last chance to gather full-throttle data, which can be very useful later in eliminations.

43. Breakout losses

Logging the number of races you've lost due to a breakout will help you fine tune your dial-in skills.

44. Breakout wins

Same as above, only now you're recording the races you've won where a breakout was involved.

45. First or last

Did you get to the finish line first or tap the brake pedal and let your opponent get there first? Make a notation here so you'll know. As with most of the data on this chart, you can identify trends and make adjustments by analyzing your results. For example, if you're getting to the finish line

first but losing a high number of runs via a breakout, you probably need to make an adjustment to your dial-in strategy.

46. Fouls

Every time you leave before the green light, whether during a time trial or elimination run, you should make a note if it. Afterwards, you can compare this data with other statistics such as time of day, left or right lane, staged status, etc., to identify and correct problems.

47. True-win margin measured in time

The true-win margin, which is the margin of victory separating the winner and loser of each race at the finish line, is noted at the bottom of each time slip and should be cataloged. Consider this a report card that grades your finish-line driving.

48. True-win margin measured in distance

Using the formula described elsewhere in this chapter, you can easily convert your MOV (margin of victory) into distance as measured in feet and inches. Again, by monitoring this statistic, you can greatly improve your finish-line skills.

49. Expenses

Every time you head to the track, you should track your expenses including fuel, tires, entry fees, food, and lodging. This information can be extremely useful at tax time.

50. Winnings

In addition to your expenses, you should keep track of any prize money won, not just for bragging rights but also for accounting purposes. While it's possible that all or part of your racing operation can be

tax deductible, it's also possible, depending on where you live, that all or part of your winnings may be taxable as income.

Useful Formulas

The following are some handy charts and formulas that every racer should have at his or her disposal:

Cubic inch displacement (CID)
CID = bore x bore x stroke x 0.7854
x number of cylinders
Example: 4.5 x 4.5 x 3.75 x 0.7854
x 8 = 477.103 ci

HP and torque
HP = RPM x torque / 5,252
Example: 8,500 rpm x 500 ft-lbs torque
/ 5,252 = 809.215 hp

Torque = 5,252 x hp / RPM
Example: 5,252 x 809.215 / 8,500
= 500 ft-lbs torque

Rear gear ratio
Rear gear ratio = RPM at finish line
x tire diameter / MPH x 336
Example: 6,200 x 30.5 / 115 x 336
= 5.52 gear ratio

Compression ratio
Compression ratio = combustion chamber cc's + head gasket cc + deck cubic in cc + displacement x 2.0483

Weights

Oil: 1 gal = 7.0 lbs
1 qt = 1.75 lbs

Gasoline: 1 gal = 6.2 lbs
1 qt = 1.55 lbs

Water: 1 gal = 8.4 lbs
1 qt = 2.10 lbs

GLOSSARY OF DRAG RACING TERMS

Alternate: A driver whose ET was not quick enough to earn a position in a qualified field. Although officially a non-qualifier, an alternate could be inserted into a qualified field to replace a qualified driver who is unable to report for eliminations on race day.

Backed into: Slang terminology used by bracket racers to describe a driving technique where one competitor brakes near the end of the course in order to cross the finish line first but by the smallest possible margin. Related phrases include "closed it up" and "tightened it up."

Back half: The second half of the race course. In quarter-mile racing, the last 660 feet of the racetrack is the back half, and in eighth-mile racing, the last 330 feet is the back half. A comparison of back-half ETs is often a good indicator of a vehicle's HP.

Blinder: A panel used at some drag strips that is placed in the center of the Christmas-tree starting system, and is designed to shield each side of the tree from view from the opponent's lane.

Bracket racing: A popular form of drag racing, which allows vehicles of differing performance levels to compete on an equal basis by allowing a slower vehicle to receive a handicap start. The breakout rule is also enforced, meaning that a driver who runs quicker than his or her predicted ET (dial-in) is eliminated. Bracket racing places an emphasis on driver skill rather than raw speed.

Break out: Recording an ET quicker than the posted dial-in or common index during eliminations, resulting in disqualification. If both contestants in a race break out, the winner is the driver who broke out by the smallest margin.

Bump spot: The ET of the last driver in a qualified field (i.e., the 16th position in a field open to only the 16 quickest qualifiers), precarious in that, if bettered by a driver currently not qualified, the No. 16 qualifier can be "bumped" out of the field.

Bump down: A method of adjusting a driver's reaction time immediately after the delay box/transmission-brake button has been released. For example, a driver who has released his or her transmission-brake button too late and quickly realizes the error may quickly use the "bump down" feature to subtract a set amount of delay in order to achieve the desired reaction time.

Burned piston: A melted or damaged piston often caused by extreme heat, which is the result of a lack of fuel within the cylinder.

Burnout: A pre-race exercise that involves spinning the tires behind the starting line in order to clean and heat them in an effort to enhance traction.

Burndown: A psychological battle between two drivers in which each refuses to fully stage for a race. Generally, the objective of a burndown is to break an opponent's concentration prior to a race.

Buy-back: A paid re-entry into competition after a loss in the early rounds of a race. Many tracks permit buy-backs as late as the second round of competition.

Christmas tree: The electronic starting device usually placed in the center of the track, which begins each race utilizing a sequential countdown of lights.

Chute: Slang for parachute. A chute is usually used to assist high-speed braking in vehicles running in excess of 150 mph.

Clutch dust: A thick black haze, which emanates from the rear of many professional-class race cars. It is the normal by-product of the friction and erosion of clutch discs.

Competition license: A credential issued to competitors who meet all requirements to drive in a specific class or eliminator category. Qualifications for a Competition License often include a thorough physical examination, and the successful completion of runs observed by officials and licensed peers.

Competition number: The identification of a drag racing driver displayed prominently on each vehicle entered in a race. Unlike most other forms of motorsports, a drag-racing competition number identifies the driver rather than the car.

Dead-on: An ET that exactly matches the driver's dial-in or index to the hundredth of a second. Dead-on runs that match the dial-in or index to the thousandth of a second are considered perfect.

Deep stage: A procedure in which a driver positions their vehicle slightly over the starting line, rolling far enough to turn off the top stage light on the Christmas tree. Note that this practice is not legal in all forms of competition.

Delay box: A device designed to improve reaction time, which permits a driver to initiate the run by releasing a button by hand at the first flash of the Christmas-tree lights. Using a delay box, drivers may fine tune their reaction times to within a thousandth of a second.

Dial-in: Used in bracket racing, a dial-in is a competitor's prediction of his or vehicle's ET, which is used to establish a handicap. The term dial-in is derived from the earliest handicapping computers. These quarter-mile times or dial-ins were manually entered using thumbwheel dials.

Dial-under: Similar to a dial-in, but used by competitors in Super Stock and Stock racing who compete on a fixed index. In those classes, competitors may choose a dial-in that is lower than their assigned class index.

Diaper: A restraint device made from ballistic and/or absorbent material that surrounds the lower portions of the engine and serves as a containment device in the event of a damaged engine or a loss of fluids.

Dropped cylinder: A condition most often seen in Top Fuel dragsters and nitro Funny Cars, in which a spark plug fails to ignite, substantially decreasing total power output. A dropped cylinder is often distinguishable by raw fuel spewing from an exhaust header.

Dump: The act in which a sportsman category racer, unable to catch his or her opponent, gives up the pursuit at the last possible moment, hitting the brakes in an effort to force an opponent to break out.

Elapsed Time (ET): The electronically timed duration of a run from start to finish. Modern computer timers can accurately record an ET to within one millionth of a second, (0.000001).

Eliminator: A category of racing in which drivers compete under a common set of rules and regulations. Examples include Top Fuel eliminator, Pro Stock eliminator, and Super Gas eliminator.

Eliminations: The portion of an event that determines a race winner through a tournament of individual contests in which each loser is expelled, or eliminated, from further competition and the winner advances to the next round.

Fire bottles: Another term for fire extinguishers that are carried onboard a race car and activated by the driver in the event of a fire.

Foot racer: Also known as a foot-brake racer, this slang term describes a sportsman-class competitor who does not use a delay box or transmission brake in his or her car, preferring to rely on just the throttle and brake pedal to control the vehicle at the starting line.

Fuel check: A process where a fuel sample is inspected to ensure its contents fall within limits permitted for each individual class.

Fuel injection: A system designed to direct fuel into each engine cylinder. Fuel injection replaced carburetion as the standard in air/fuel management for production cars during the early 1980s and it is widely used in many drag racing applications.

Full tree: A starting sequence produced on the Christmas tree where contestants view a countdown of three amber signals and a green starting light at 0.500-second intervals.

Handicap: The difference between the dial-in or indexes of two contestants, which, when entered into the Christmas tree's computer, will be translated to a head start for the slower competitor.

Heads-up: An elimination round in which neither competitor is given a handicap. Although these even-start contests are the standard in all professional categories and in all divisions utilizing a common index, they sometimes occur in other classes when contestants happen to choose identical dial-ins or when two sportsman vehicles of identical classification meet in competition.

Hemi: An engine utilizing a hemispherical-shaped combustion chamber. Hemi engines are the standard in the Top Fuel and Funny Car divisions.

Holeshot: A reaction-time advantage gained by a driver who left the starting line before his or her opponent.

Index: A theoretical ET used to handicap or qualify sportsman racers. Specific classes are assigned an index, which represents what a well-prepared vehicle should run. Similar to golf's par system, an index must be met or exceeded to ensure competitiveness.

Ladder: The eliminations-pairing schedule based on qualifying position. Two different formats are generally used. In professional categories, superior qualifying performance is rewarded with a slower opponent in the opening round of the race. For example, a 16-car qualified field would include the pairing of the quickest (No.1) qualifier racing against the slowest (No. 16) qualifier while No. 2 faces No. 15, etc. In sportsman racing, a 16-car ladder would feature the No. 1 qualifier paired with the No. 9 qualifier while No. 2 raced against No. 10, etc.

Lane choice: The option to determine the racing lane to be used for competition, earned via a quicker ET in the previous round of qualifying or eliminations.

Match racer: A competitor who earns income as a featured attraction at an event.

Mountain motor: A large-displacement engine (generally considered 600 ci or larger), originally named for the pioneers of Pro Stock racing who sometimes produced illegally large engines.

National standard: A synonym for index.

Over-staged: Occurs when a vehicle's

front wheels accidentally roll completely past the starting line while the driver is attempting to stage.

Package: A slang term that indicates a driver's performance. A package is determined by adding the driver's reaction time to the vehicle's ET in relationship to its dial-in. For example, a contestant recording a reaction time of 0.003 second while clocking a 10.154-second ET against a 10.15-second dial-in would have achieved a 0.007-second package, meaning that an opponent's opportunity to win would be only 0.006 second.

Perfect run: An extremely rare occurrence in which a competitor records a perfect 0.000 reaction time while also clocking a perfect ET against his or her dial-in, resulting in a 0.000-second package.

Pre-staged: A position on the racetrack used to alert a competitor that he or she is approaching the starting line. When a driver reaches the pre-stage area, the top yellow light on the Christmas tree will illuminate, indicating that the competitor's front tires are just a few inches from the starting line.

Pro tree: A starting sequence produced on the Christmas tree in which contestants view a simultaneous flash of all three amber signals followed 0.400 second later by the green starting light. This start method is used in all professional categories as well as sportsman eliminators in which a common index is utilized.

Progressive times: A series of ETs and speeds recorded at specified distances on the race track, normally at the 60-foot, 330-foot, 660-foot, and 1,000-foot distances. A progressive speed reading is also usually supplied at the halfway (660-foot) point of the track.

Reaction time: The electronically measured response of a driver and vehicle to the green starting light. Although considered the true measurement of a driver's reflexes, it also gauges the responsiveness of the vehicle's engine and chassis. A 0.000-second reaction time is considered perfect on either a full-tree start or a pro-tree start.

Red-light: A disqualification that occurs when a driver leaves the starting line before the green starting light illuminates, which triggers a red-light at the bottom of the Christmas tree.

Rev limiter: A device that restricts the total RPM capability of the engine, usually by disrupting the firing capability of the ignition at a pre-set RPM level. A rev limiter is used primarily to minimize potential engine damage from excessive RPM, although a rev limiter is also used to maintain a consistent RPM level during the initial launch from the starting line.

Round: The completion of racing for all competitors remaining in a specific eliminator. Each successive round of racing features the winning half of all contestants from the previous round.

Sandbagging: A bracket racing technique where a driver intentionally selects a dial-in that is slower than his or her car's capability, allowing the driver to remain ahead of an opponent through the run until braking to slow the car just before the finish line. Also known as "bagging" and "dialing soft."

Sportsman: Generally used to describe an amateur or hobby racer. Also used to describe a racer who does not use racing as a primary source of income. Most forms of Sportsman racing, including bracket racing, utilize a handicapped start or a common elapsed-time index as the basis of competition.

Stripe: Slang term for the finish line.

Staged: The position on the race track of the actual starting line; once a vehicle's front tires break the light beam located at the staged line, a small yellow bulb is illuminated on the Christmas tree signifying that the vehicle is positioned correctly in order for the race to begin.

Staging lanes: The area of the drag strip directly adjacent to the racetrack, which is used to organize and pair racers prior to qualifying sessions or eliminations.

Starter: The designated official whose duties include activating the Christmas-tree starting system, inspecting and maintaining the condition of the starting-line area, and watching each race for potential on-track rules infractions.

Supercharger: A specialized compressor, traditionally mounted on top of an engine and driven by a belt connected to the crankshaft, which forces air and fuel into the engine to dramatically increase power output. Also known as a "blower" or "huffer."

Teardown: A random vehicle inspection by race officials during an event to ensure required specifications and rules are being met by competitors. Competitors who are asked to submit to a teardown must often disassemble their engine for a thorough inspection of internal components.

Throttle stop: This component helps drivers intentionally slow their vehicle by using an adjustable timer to open and close the throttle for a pre-determined length of time. Throttle stops are used primarily in the Super classes where racers are attempting to hit a fixed index.

Time trial: A practice run that is usually performed prior to the start of actual competition. Time trials are used by sportsman division competitors to determine dial-ins used in eliminations.

Tire shake: A severe vibration that occurs usually during hard acceleration when a tire attempts to run over itself or is severely distorted.

True-win margin: The actual distance between two vehicles as measured at the finish line. The true-win margin is reported as an ET, although it can easily be converted into a measurement of distance.

Water box: The area located behind the starting line that is the designated area for pre-race burnouts; also known as a burnout box.

NOTES	RUN 1	RUN 2	RUN 3	RUN 4
Oil/Number of Runs				
Valvelash				
Timing				
Jetting				
T-Stop RPM/Ratio				
Converter/Stall				
Starting Line RPM				
Shift RPM/Time				
Exhaust Temperature				
Shock Settings	Front Rear	Front Rear	Front Rear	Front Rear
Wheelie Bar Height				
Gear Ratio	Trans Rear End	Trans Rear End	Trans Rear End	Trans Rear End
Tires/# of Runs				
Ballast	Front Middle Rear	Front Middle Rear	Front Middle Rear	Front Middle Rear
Vehicle Weight				

NOTES	RUN 1	RUN 2	RUN 3	RUN 4
Oil/Number of Runs				
Valvelash				
Timing				
Jetting				
T-Stop RPM/Ratio				
Converter/Stall				
Starting Line RPM				
Shift RPM/Time				
Exhaust Temperature				
Shock Settings	Front Rear	Front Rear	Front Rear	Front Rear
Wheelie Bar Height				
Gear Ratio	Trans Rear End	Trans Rear End	Trans Rear End	Trans Rear End
Tires/# of Runs				
Ballast	Front Middle Rear	Front Middle Rear	Front Middle Rear	Front Middle Rear
Vehicle Weight				

NOTES	RUN 1	RUN 2	RUN 3	RUN 4
Oil/Number of Runs				
Valvelash				
Timing				
Jetting				
T-Stop RPM/Ratio				
Converter/Stall				
Starting Line RPM				
Shift RPM/Time				
Exhaust Temperature				
Shock Settings	Front Rear	Front Rear	Front Rear	Front Rear
Wheelie Bar Height				
Gear Ratio	Trans Rear End	Trans Rear End	Trans Rear End	Trans Rear End
Tires/# of Runs				
Ballast	Front Middle Rear	Front Middle Rear	Front Middle Rear	Front Middle Rear
Vehicle Weight				

DATA SHEET

Event:_____   Points Earned:_____
Date:_____   Computer Code:_____

DATA	1	2	3	4	5	6	7	8	9	10	11	12
Time of Day												
Sunny/Cloudy/Dark												
Lane												
Time Run/Elimination												
Reaction Time												
Delay												
Reaction Time Bump												
60 ft. ET												
330 ft. ET												
660 ft. ET												
660 ft. MPH												
1000 ft. ET												
1320 ft. ET												
1320 ft. MPH												
60-330 ft. ET												
330-660 ft. ET												
660-1000 ft. ET												
1000-1320 ft. ET												
Dial-In												
Actual ET												
Predicted ET												
Throttle Stop Setting												
Delay Box Setting												
Air Temperature												
Humidity												
Vapor Pressure												
Barometric Pressure												
Air Density												
Corrected Altitude												
Correction Factor												
Track Temperature												
Wind Speed												
Wind Direction												
Tire PSI Front												
Tire PSI Rear												

FIND A TRACK NEAR YOU

Go to the Member Track Locator feature at NHRA.com or pick up the latest edition of *National DRAGSTER* to find the NHRA Member Track nearest you.

The Best Team in Drag Racing

- **Go to NHRA.com for all the latest events and information**
- **Join NHRA and enjoy all the benefits**
    - Weekly expanded coverage of NHRA Drag Racing in *National DRAGSTER*
    - Live event audio broadcasts
    - NHRA Rulebook and $485,000 excess medical insurance coverage*

NHRA NORTHEAST DIVISION
Northeast Div. Dir.: Bob Lang
Telephone: (215) 343-2558
E-mail: blang@nhra.com

Includes NHRA Member Tracks in: Connecticut, Delaware, District of Columbia, Maine, Maryland, Massachusetts, New Hampshire, New Jersey, New York, Pennsylvania, Rhode Island, Vermont, Virginia, West Virginia, and Maritime Provinces, Eastern Ontario, and Quebec, Canada

---

NHRA SOUTHEAST DIVISION
Southeast Div. Dir.: Bill Holt
Telephone: (352) 374-9922
E-mail: bholt@nhra.com

Includes NHRA Member Tracks in: Alabama, Florida, Georgia, North Carolina, South Carolina, Tennessee, Puerto Rico, and the Caribbean

---

NHRA NORTH CENTRAL DIVISION
North Central Div. Dir.: Jay Hullinger
Telephone: (765) 689-8727
E-mail: jhullinger@nhra.com

Includes NHRA Member Tracks in: Illinois, Indiana, Kentucky, Michigan, Ohio, Wisconsin, and Western Ontario, Canada

---

NHRA SOUTH CENTRAL DIVISION
South Central Div. Dir.: Craig Hutchinson
Telephone: (936) 539-4474
E-mail: chutchinson@nhra.com

Includes NHRA Member Tracks in: Arkansas, Louisiana, Mississippi, New Mexico, Oklahoma, Texas, and Mexico

---

NHRA WEST CENTRAL DIVISION
West Central Div. Dir.: Rob Park
Telephone: (816) 795-8055
E-mail: rpark@nhra.com

Includes NHRA Member Tracks in: Colorado, Iowa, Kansas, Minnesota, Missouri, Nebraska, North Dakota, Wyoming, and Manitoba, Canada

---

NHRA NORTHWEST DIVISION
Northwest Div. Dir.: Jonathan Adams
Telephone: (253) 826-8666
E-mail: jadams@nhra.com

Includes NHRA Member Tracks in: Alaska, Idaho, Montana, Oregon, Washington, and Alberta, British Columbia, and Saskatchewan, Canada

---

NHRA PACIFIC DIVISION
Pacific Div. Dir.: Mike Rice
Telephone: (626) 914-4761 ext. 272
E-mail: mrice@nhra.com

Includes NHRA Member Tracks in: Arizona, California, Hawaii, Nevada, Utah, and Baja California, Mexico

---

*Go to www.NHRA.com/insurance for important details about insurance coverage limitations.

APPENDIX E: RELEASE AND WAIVER AGREEMENT

RELEASE AND WAIVER OF LIABILITY, ASSUMPTION OF RISK AND INDEMNITY AGREEMENT

_____   _____
NAME OF TRACK AND/OR EVENTS   EVENT DATE(S)

IN CONSIDERATION of being permitted to compete, officiate, observe, work for, or participate in any way in the EVENT(S) or being permitted to enter for any purpose any RESTRICTED AREA (defined as the advance staging area, burn out area, competition area, shutdown area, staging lanes, return road area, and any other area within the barriers, fences, and/or structures separating the general public from racing activities), EACH OF THE UNDERSIGNED, for himself/herself, his/her personal representatives, heirs, and next of kin.

1. Acknowledges, agrees, and represents that he/she has or will immediately upon entering any such RESTRICTED AREAS, and will continuously thereafter, inspect the RESTRICTED AREAS which he/she enters and he/she further agrees and warrants that, if at any time, he/she is in or about RESTRICTED AREAS and he/she feels anything to be unsafe, he/she will immediately advise the officials of such and will leave the RESTRICTED AREAS and/or refuse to participate further in the EVENT(S).

2. HEREBY RELEASES, WAIVES, DISCHARGES AND COVENANTS NOT TO SUE the promoters, participants, racing associations, sanctioning organizations or any affiliated entities thereof, track operators, track owners, officials, car owners, drivers, pit crews, rescue personnel, any persons in any RESTRICTED AREA, promoters, sponsors, equipment and parts manufacturers and suppliers, advertisers, owners and lessees of premises used to conduct the EVENT(S), premises and event inspectors, surveyors, underwriters/brokers, consultants and others who give recommendations, directions, or instructions or engage in risk evaluation or loss control activities regarding the premises or EVENT(S) and for each of them, their directors, officers, agents, and employees, all for the purposes herein referred to as "Releasees" FROM ALL LIABILITY TO THE UNDERSIGNED, his/her personal representatives, assigns, heirs, and next of kin, FOR ANY AND ALL LOSS OR DAMAGE, AND ANY CLAIM OR DEMANDS THEREFORE ON ACCOUNT OF INJURY TO THE PERSON OR PROPERTY OR RESULTING IN DEATH OF THE UNDERSIGNED ARISING OUT OF OR RELATED TO THE EVENT(S), WHETHER CAUSED BY THE NEGLIGENCE OF THE RELEASEES OR OTHERWISE.

3. HEREBY AGREES TO INDEMNIFY AND SAVE AND HOLD HARMLESS the RELEASEES and each of them FROM ANY LOSS, LIABILITY, DAMAGE, OR COST they may incur arising out of or related in any manner to my attendance at or participation in the EVENT(S) and WHETHER CAUSED BY THE NEGLIGENCE OF THE RELEASEES OR OTHERWISE.

4. HEREBY ASSUMES FULL RESPONSIBILITY FOR ANY RISK OF BODILY INJURY, DEATH OR PROPERTY DAMAGE arising out of or related to the EVENT(S) whether caused by the NEGLIGENCE OF THE RELEASEES OR OTHERWISE.

5. HEREBY acknowledges that THE ACTIVITIES OF THE EVENT(S) ARE VERY DANGEROUS and involve the risk of serious injury and/or property damage. Each of THE UNDERSIGNED also expressly acknowledges that INJURIES RECEIVED MAY BE COMPOUNDED OR INCREASED BY NEGLIGENT RESCUE OPERATIONS OR PROCEDURES OF THE RELEASEES.

6. HEREBY agrees that this Release and Waiver of Liability, Assumption of Risk and Indemnity Agreement extends to all acts of negligence by the RELEASEES, INCLUDING NEGLIGENT RESCUE OPERATIONS and is intended to be as broad and inclusive as is permitted by the laws of the Province or State in which the Event(s) is/are conducted and that if any portion thereof is held invalid, it is agreed that the balance shall, notwithstanding, continue in full legal force and effect.

I HAVE READ THIS RELEASE AND WAIVER OF LIABILITY, ASSUMPTION OF RISK AND INDEMNITY AGREEMENT, FULLY UNDERSTAND ITS TERMS, UNDERSTAND THAT I HAVE GIVEN UP SUBSTANTIAL RIGHTS BY SIGNING IT, AND HAVE SIGNED IT FREELY AND VOLUNTARILY WITHOUT ANY INDUCEMENT, ASSURANCE OR GUARANTEE BEING MADE TO ME AND INTEND MY SIGNATURE TO BE A COMPLETE AND UNCONDITIONAL RELEASE OF ALL LIABILITY TO THE GREATEST EXTENT ALLOWED BY LAW. I ACKNOWLEDGE AND AGREE THAT FAILURE TO WITNESS THIS AGREEMENT SHALL NOT AFFECT ITS VALIDITY.

PRINT NAME	SIGN NAME HERE	PRINT NAME	SIGN NAME HERE
	I HAVE READ THIS RELEASE		I HAVE READ THIS RELEASE
	I HAVE READ THIS RELEASE		I HAVE READ THIS RELEASE
	I HAVE READ THIS RELEASE		I HAVE READ THIS RELEASE
	I HAVE READ THIS RELEASE		I HAVE READ THIS RELEASE
	I HAVE READ THIS RELEASE		I HAVE READ THIS RELEASE
	I HAVE READ THIS RELEASE		I HAVE READ THIS RELEASE
	I HAVE READ THIS RELEASE		I HAVE READ THIS RELEASE
	I HAVE READ THIS RELEASE		I HAVE READ THIS RELEASE
	I HAVE READ THIS RELEASE		I HAVE READ THIS RELEASE
	I HAVE READ THIS RELEASE		I HAVE READ THIS RELEASE

OFFICIAL USE ONLY

_____   _____
Signature and Title of Witness   Address of Witness

WMS-DRAG (EDITION 6)

MORE GREAT TITLES AVAILABLE FROM CARTECH®

Additional books that may interest you...

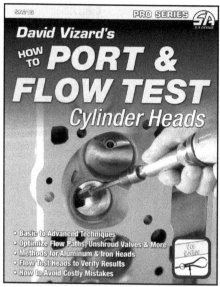
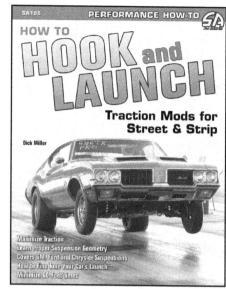
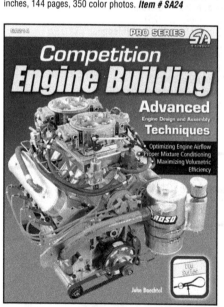